THE
HOUSE OF
COMPREHENSION

THE HOUSE OF COMPREHENSION

CONSTANCE D. CASSERLY

COMPASS

The House of Comprehension

Copyright © 2013 by Constance D. Casserly

Published by Compass, an imprint of Brigantine Media
211 North Avenue, Saint Johnsbury, Vermont 05819

Cover and book design by Jacob L. Grant

ISBN 978-1-9384061-7-1

For more information about other Compass books, visit
www.compasspublishing.org

Brigantine Media
211 North Avenue
Saint Johnsbury, Vermont 05819
Phone: 802-751-8802
Fax: 802-751-8804
E-mail: neil@brigantinemedia.com

DEDICATION

This book is dedicated to

the catalyst for this project,

my mother,

Mary G. Neal
(1916-2012)

- - - - - - - - - - - - - - - -

ACKNOWLEDGMENTS

After I designed the blueprint for *The House of Comprehension*, many people who saw it understood the need it would fill for teachers. Neil Raphel and Janis Raye of Brigantine Media grasped its possibilities and welcomed it into the Compass Publishing home. Janis's critiques, insightful suggestions and editing prowess transformed my literature comprehension program, strategies and activities into a substantive structure for English Language Arts teachers. Jacob Grant, the Media Director at Compass, made the book's concept come alive with his awesome graphics.

My mother, Mary Neal (1916-2012), planted the seeds for this project with her fervent suggestion that I share my teaching ideas with my colleagues. My husband, Tim, my children, Kimberly and Matthew, and my classroom friends and colleagues shared her belief in my vision and motivated me with their support.

To all of you, I send a heart bursting with gratitude.

CONTENTS

54.6

53.5

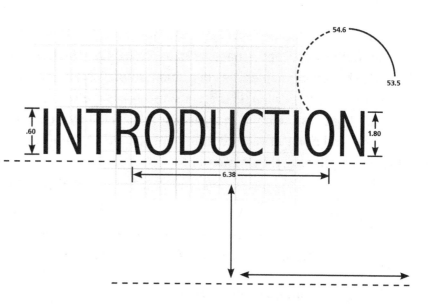

INTRODUCTION

Once upon a time, three pigs built separate houses. Pig A constructed his of straw. The Big Bad Wolf blew it down. Pig B erected his of twigs. Once again the Big Bad Wolf destroyed it with a few blusters of breath. Then Pig C tried his hand at building a house. He mortared brick on top of brick. This time, the Big Bad Wolf wasted his breath.

Pig C laughed and laughed, reveling in his understanding of structure, while the wolf collapsed in his front yard, his lungs as deflated as popped balloons. Pig C understood how *all* of the parts of a house join forces to create a substantial whole.

English Language Arts teachers work hard to help students understand structure in literature to build strong academic houses like Pig C's, not fragile ones like those of Pig A and Pig B. Durable houses of comprehension expand knowledge, enhance perception of the structure of texts, and develop strong reading skills that will last students a lifetime.

Think of the elements of literature—character, plot/conflict, setting, theme, symbols, point of view, and tone—as the framework of a house. What is the character of the house? Is it an A-frame, a two-story colonial, a thatched roof cottage, a mid-century ranch, or a Tudor mansion? Evaluate the setting: is the house in the desert, a city, the prairie, or nestled on a mountainside? Does it have an oceanfront view, look out onto a suburban development, or is it shaded by maple trees in a small town? When you enter the house, you begin to see the plot—the floor plan. Is there a smooth flow to the rooms? Can the occupants grow and thrive? The details embellish the interior design. They create a tone, suggest a theme, and use symbols and point of view to round out the structure of the dwelling. After all, every house, like a story, does make a statement.

The House of Comprehension program helps teachers and students:

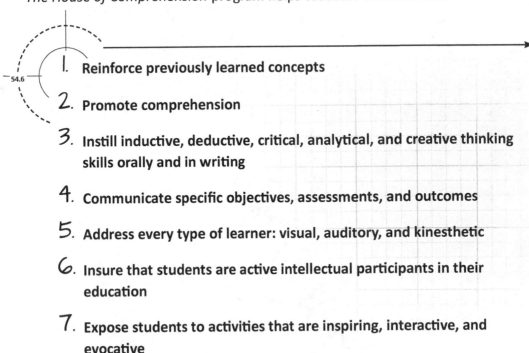

1. **Reinforce previously learned concepts**

2. **Promote comprehension**

3. **Instill inductive, deductive, critical, analytical, and creative thinking skills orally and in writing**

4. **Communicate specific objectives, assessments, and outcomes**

5. **Address every type of learner: visual, auditory, and kinesthetic**

6. **Insure that students are active intellectual participants in their education**

7. **Expose students to activities that are inspiring, interactive, and evocative**

Closing the achievement gap between students who work at or above grade level and those who perform below level is a key goal for educators. The activities in this book enable teachers to reach both proficient and non-proficient students and to help them all advance their skill levels. These lessons prove that learning can be invigorating. They never fail to initiate stimulating small and large group discussions and clear, focused writing.

Most states have adopted the Common Core Standards. The lessons in The House of Comprehension were created to insure that students meet or exceed the knowledge, skills, and understanding of the elements of literature and the writing proficiency that they must demonstrate. When teachers integrate these activities into their plans along with their own assignments and assessments, they can be assured that they are addressing the following Common Core Standards:

Reading Standards for Literature and Informational Text

• Key Ideas and Details
• Craft and Structure
• Integration of Knowledge and Ideas
• Range of Reading and Level of Text Complexity

Writing Standards

• Text Types and Purposes
• Production and Distribution of Writing
• Research to Build and Present Knowledge
• Range of Writing

Language Standards

• Conventions of Standard English
• Knowledge of Language
• Vocabulary Acquisition and Use

Speaking & Listening Standards

• Comprehension and Collaboration
• Presentation of Knowledge and Ideas

Each one of the activities addresses one or more Common Core Standards. Together, they form a solid Common Core foundation by presenting students with multiple opportunities to advance their abilities, skills, and comprehension. Charts at the end of this section show all the activities that can be used to teach each Common Core Standard.

Using the elements of literature as building blocks, students and the teacher embrace the hierarchy of Bloom's Taxonomy. They *remember and understand* what they note, *apply* that understanding along with their prior knowledge by asking questions as well as by comparing and contrasting, *analyze* the various components they encounter, *evaluate* how each element connects to and enhances the others, and *synthesize* all of the information they gather. They understand that if the story is to provide a solid structure, it must contain *all* of the elements of literature.

Students will learn to distinguish between and understand the importance of every component. They will recognize that the story and the elements create a durable whole by working together. Incorporating each of these factors into the study of any book will enable students to explain, orally and in writing, whether any story creates a house of straw, of twigs, or of bricks.

The House of Comprehension offers teachers a practical, flexible, and complete program that enriches their students' education and enables learners to build resilient academic houses that will survive any Big Bad Wolf.

COMMON CORE STANDARDS

TEACHER NOTES

- The numbers of the Anchor Standards give a broad view, but each one corresponds with a grade-specific number. The Anchor Standards condense the information; i.e., R1 is a reduced version of RL1 and RI1.

- For the full-length versions, teachers can refer to each grade-specific Standard. http://www.corestandards.org/ela-literacy

Key Ideas and Details

R1. Read closely to determine what the text says explicitly and to make logical inferences from it; cite specific textual evidence when writing or speaking to support conclusions drawn from the text.

R2. Determine central ideas or themes of a text and analyze their development; summarize the key supporting details and ideas.

R3. Analyze how and why individuals, events, and ideas develop and interact over the course of a text.

Craft and Structure

R4. Interpret words and phrases as they are used in a text, including determining technical, connotative, and figurative meanings, and analyze how specific word choices shape meaning or tone.

Aha! So This Is What It's About! (p. 55)   *Symbols Hold the Key (p. 120)*
Green Light! Red Light! (p. 96)   *Symbols: They Represent! (p. 124)*
Journal Response Letters (p. 99)   *Let's Tone Up (p. 137)*
What Was I Thinking? (p. 102)   *Story Review (p. 145)*

R5. Analyze the structure of texts, including how specific sentences, paragraphs, and larger portions of the text (e.g., a section, chapter, scene, or stanza) relate to each other and the whole.

Green Light! Red Light! (p. 96)   *What Was I Thinking? (p. 102)*
Journal Response Letters (p. 99)

R6. Assess how point of view or purpose shapes the content and style of a text.

Green Light! Red Light! (p. 96)   *Starring...ME! (p. 132)*
Journal Response Letters (p. 99)   *Let's Tone Up (p. 137)*
What's Your Point? (p. 126)   *Story Review (p. 145)*

Integration of Knowledge and Ideas

R7. Integrate and evaluate content presented in diverse formats and media, including visually and quantitatively, as well as in words.

If the Theme Fits... Use It! (p. 117)

R8. Delineate and evaluate the argument and specific claims in a text, including the validity of the reasoning as well as the relevance and sufficiency of the evidence.

Symbols: They Represent! (p. 124)

R9. Analyze how two or more texts address similar themes or topics in order to build knowledge or to compare the approaches the authors take.

What's In a Theme? (p. 113)   *Symbols Hold the Key (p. 120)*
If the Theme Fits...Use It!   (p. 117)

Range of Reading and Level of Text Complexity

R10. Read and comprehend complex literary and informational texts independently and proficiently.

What's the Conflict? (p. 80)   *Symbols: They Represent! (p. 124)*
What's In a Theme? (p. 113)   *Starring...ME! (p. 132)*
If the Theme Fits...Use It! (p. 117)   *Let's Tone Up (p. 137)*
Symbols Hold the Key (p. 120)

Text Types and Purposes

W1. Write arguments to support claims in an analysis of substantive topics or texts, using valid reasoning and relevant and sufficient evidence.

W2. Write informative/explanatory texts to examine and convey complex ideas and information clearly and accurately through the effective selection, organization, and analysis of content.

W3. Write narratives to develop real or imagined experiences or events using effective technique, well-chosen details, and well-structured event sequences.

Comprehension and Collaboration

SL1. Prepare for and participate effectively in a range of conversations and collaborations with diverse partners, building on others' ideas and expressing their own clearly and persuasively.

SL2. Integrate and evaluate information presented in diverse media and formats, including visually, quantitatively, and orally.

SL3. Evaluate a speaker's point of view, reasoning, and use of evidence and rhetoric.

Presentation of Knowledge and Ideas

SL4. Present information, findings, and supporting evidence such that listeners can follow the line of reasoning and the organization, development, and style are appropriate to task, purpose, and audience.

Conventions of Standard English

L1. Demonstrate command of the conventions of standard English grammar and usage when writing or speaking.

L2. Demonstrate command of the conventions of standard English capitalization, punctuation, and spelling when writing.

TIMING OF ACTIVITIES

The activities in *The House of Comprehension* are keyed to the timing as you work through a piece of literature. Some of the activities work best when you start teaching the new piece of literature, while others work better as students study the literature further. This list shows you when each activity in the book is appropriate for use.

Exposition

Inciting Moment

Rising Action

   (Use this anytime between the latter part of the Rising Action and the Falling Action)

   (Start this activity during the latter part of the Rising Action. Students can add to it through the Resolution.)

   (Introduce this during the latter part of the Rising Action, but before the Climax.)

Climax

   (Although this works well when students analyze the Rising Action situations, it is an excellent way for students to analyze the protagonist's choice in the climactic situation.)

Falling Action

   (Use this when enough information exists to analyze the story for theme—during the Falling Action or Resolution.)

   (Use this activity either in the Falling Action or during the Resolution, but AFTER the *What's In a Theme?* activity.)

Resolution

Throughout the Piece of Literature

These activities can be used when teachers introduce an element, or whenever they want to check students' comprehension

After the Piece of Literature is Completed

For Any Reading Selection at Any Time

CHAPTER 1

THE BLUEPRINTS

Lesson plans that lead to success achieve a number of goals: they communicate specific assessments and outcomes, they include clear teacher-led and student-centered activities, and they offer the opportunity for students to accept ownership of their work.

When teachers create lesson plans for analyzing literature, they should think like architects. They are drawing the blueprints for each student's house of comprehension. There are two lesson-planning tools in this chapter that help teachers organize their instruction for each piece of literature they study throughout the year. Teachers should start the planning of every new literature unit using these two charts: **Unit Structure** and **Activities Plan**.

Lesson design must take into account local, state, and federal requirements, as well as the school district's literature program of studies. Literature lessons reinforce previously learned concepts, promote comprehension, and instill deductive, critical, and analytic thinking skills, both orally and in writing.

Teachers must consider student proficiency levels and learning styles as they plan. Every student will exhibit right, left, or whole-brain tendencies in how they learn, depending on the subject area. Activities must address the issues of auditory, kinesthetic, and visual learners. Special Education children are often merged into mainstream classes, and their particular needs must also be addressed.

Teachers must also consider *how* they want to cover the facts and ideas they present. They need to offer activities where students can hear, read, think, write, speak, and do as often as possible. Studies have shown that within a week, students forget around 80 percent of the material taught if the class offers little student involvement besides reading and listening; on the other hand, students remember material in direct proportion to the number of activities that enable them to think, to write, and to speak. When teachers choose activities that incorporate all three actions, students retain around 90 percent of the information covered. The activities in *The House of Comprehension* are designed to actively engage students in the learning process.

Teachers need to know where they want to end up before they plan the first day. Schools in most states now expect teachers to build their lessons around the Common Core Standards. By choosing which objectives to pursue for each unit, teachers will know what they want their students to accomplish before they create their daily lesson plans. The backward planning concept popularized by Grant Wiggins and Jay McTighe in their book, *Understanding by Design* (Association for Supervision and Curriculum Development, 1998), is useful for planning literature units. It allows teachers to focus their ideas and desires for their students, clarifying what they will teach and how they will teach the material.

The **Unit Structure** chart (page 20) is the tool for planning each literature unit. First, the teacher notes the objectives of the unit. The Common Core Standards to be met are listed as objectives, as well as other district or state-mandated goals. Then the teacher completes the basic information for that unit:

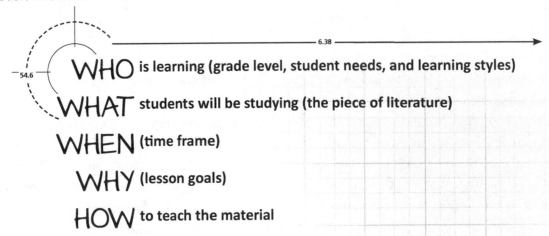

WHO is learning (grade level, student needs, and learning styles)

WHAT students will be studying (the piece of literature)

WHEN (time frame)

WHY (lesson goals)

HOW to teach the material

The **Activities Plan** (page 22) expands the "How" section of the **Unit Structure** chart. Decide which activities in this book to use with each reading assignment and fill those in the chart, along with the element of literature being taught and the part of the book that relates to the activity. The **Activities Plan** chart is created for a book of approximately 200-300 pages; all of the rows do not need to be filled in for shorter texts, and more can be added for longer books, or where teachers feel that more instruction on an element is needed.

Students who need more reinforcement in specific areas can complete more activities if necessary. Some activities can be assigned for warm-ups and homework to save class time for discussions about the book.

This method of planning works well in many ways: it is flexible, and it clarifies the tie-in between the desired objectives, the material to be studied, student needs and learning styles, and teaching methods.

Samples of each of these planning charts, **Unit Structure** (p. 20) and the **Activities Plan** (p. 22), are completed for the novel *Animal Farm,* by George Orwell.

The lesson planning charts are also very effective when teachers need to conference with administrators. They specifically show what objectives will frame the literature study as well as when and how teachers will address them. With some tweaking and explanations, the **Activities Plan** can be used to create substitute plans quickly when needed. The charts also allow for flexibility when a teacher prefers to have students work individually or in groups instead of participating in whole-class discussions, or vice versa.

UNIT STRUCTURE

General Information	Notes
Objectives	
Who	
What	
When	
Why	
How	

UNIT STRUCTURE

General Information	Notes
Objectives	
Anchor Standards: R 1, 2, 3	
Who	
8th grade regular class	Includes 5 mainstreamed SPED students; all students show a general understanding of character, plot, setting, POV, tone, but need a more thorough study of conflict, theme, symbols. Comprehension needs to be checked periodically
What	
Animal Farm (George Orwell)	
When	
October	12 85-minute block periods
Why	
Meets POS objective for studying allegory, fable, and satire as well as how the elements of literature create story framework	
How	
Directed and Constructivist Lessons/activities, assignments	Lessons on allegory, fable, satire; essay format; student manifesto project; study packets (vocabulary, study questions, journal topics)

ACTIVITIES PLAN

Novel: _____

Element of Literature	Chapters	Activities

ACTIVITIES PLAN

Novel: _Animal Farm_

Element of Literature	Chapters	Activities
Pre-Reading	1	Aha! So This Is What It's About!
Comprehension	Whole Book	Journals: Response Letters
Character	Whole Book	Time for Body Building
Character	5	Let's Second That Emotion
Character	6	Why Did You Do That?
Character	7	Fact or Opinion? You Be the Judge
Plot/Conflict	Whole Book	Plotting Along
Plot/Conflict	Whole Book	What's the Conflict?
Theme	7	What's In a Theme?
Theme	8	If the Theme Fits... Use It!
Symbols	Whole Book	Symbols Hold the Key
Symbols	Whole Book	Symbols: They Represent!
Setting	Whole Book	What Kind of World Does the Author Create?
Point of View	Whole Book	Starring...ME!
Tone	Whole Book	Let's Tone Up
Novel Review (individual)	End of Book	Character Collage
Novel Review (whole class)	End of Book	SCORE with the Literature Super Bowl

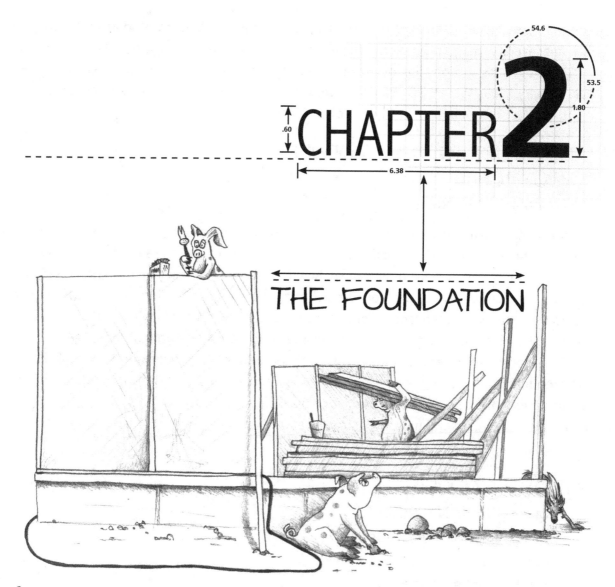

CHAPTER 2

THE FOUNDATION

Like building a house, learning starts with a strong foundation. What students already know about literature provides the foundation for the teacher to build on throughout the year. Before teachers can begin to show students how the structure of any text is composed of the elements of literature, they must assess what their students understand, and what depth of knowledge they have learned from previous teaching. By middle school, students should be familiar with all of the elements of literature in this book. Then each year, through high school, they will add complexity to their knowledge and understanding. These elements form the basis of every literature unit—short stories, books, fiction, and narrative nonfiction. Teachers can assess their students' foundation of knowledge using the activities in the **Literature Review module** in this chapter.

Students need to be able to show their comprehension of the elements of literature through their writing. When they are able to write about what they read, as well as discuss the text, teachers are best able to assess their understanding of the relationship between the elements of literature and story structure. Also, writing about literature allows teachers to address the

Common Core Writing Standards and Language Standards. The **Writing module** in this chapter includes several writing activities that should be used throughout the study of all literature units.

Every day's instruction should end with some closure activity. This chapter includes an **Exit Pass** activity (page 45), an easy way to ensure that your students take away three ideas, concepts, and/or skills with them at the end of each day.

LITERATURE REVIEW MODULE
—Analyze This!
—Analyze This! Results

Teachers need to begin each year with a review of the elements of literature to assess what students know and what they need to know. The elements of literature must be reviewed by combining them with a piece of literature. Review these elements using **Analyze This!** (page 28). For this exercise, any short story a teacher chooses will work. This allows instructors to assess the students' understanding of these components. The results will enable teachers to select which elements need to be reinforced and which need to be taught thoroughly.

The **Analyze This! Results** chart helps teachers keep track of what the students know as their foundation in the elements of literature. The simple layout of the chart helps teachers see patterns in the class to determine the critical areas of focus.

Analyze This! is useful not only as a pre-reading assessment, but also as a post-reading review.

WRITING MODULE
—Taboo Words & Phrases
—15 Days to Lose the Taboos
—Reel Them In!
—Ten Sentence Format

Teachers can use the writing activities at any point in the year, but it's best to give the **Taboo Words & Phrases** (page 32) to students as early in the term as possible. Students should be required to use it for every draft revision. This list is crucial for helping them write clear, specific sentences instead of those with meaningless, vague word choices and structure. Use the activities in **15 Days to Lose the Taboos** (page 34) to reinforce the **Taboo Words & Phrases**.

Reel Them In! (page 36) lets students practice one of the most important elements of writing—engaging the reader with a hook. Teachers can introduce this handout in a mini-lesson and have students practice writing hooks before any type of writing assignment.

The **Ten Sentence Format** (page 41) is a basic building block for students as they practice formal writing skills. Before they can write organized, coherent, and unified essays, they need to master writing the basic parts of a paragraph: the introduction (the hook, the overview or introductory statement, and the thesis statement), the body (three main ideas, each with a supporting detail), and a conclusion.

Once students master these parts, they will learn how to expand the paragraph to a complete essay that includes the same three basics: the introduction, the body, and the conclusion. Each main idea can be developed with more supporting details that can be augmented with even more particulars. This elasticity is the beauty of the **Ten Sentence Format**. Whether teachers want to require a five-paragraph essay or one with unlimited paragraphs, this format insures that students' writing has a clear focus, includes the three basic writing elements, and is organized, coherent, and unified.

Teachers should use this format for the writing exercises included in the activities, for warm-ups, and even for essay pre-writing outlines.

Why is the **Ten Sentence Format** so important?

- It reinforces the elements of a paragraph

- It offers a quick check for reading comprehension anytime teachers want a prose explanation and not a bulleted list

- It shows students how they can expand the information from paragraph format into an essay

Besides writing practice, this is also an excellent format for a quick quiz. Teachers can use the **Ten Sentence Format** as a short answer assessment during a novel study when they want to check reading comprehension and students' understanding of the element of literature under study, as well as assess the students' writing progress. For these quizzes, leave out the hook and overview statement since they are geared more for essays.

A sample of the power of the **Ten Sentence Format** follows on pages 43-44. The "Before" paragraph is an example of one students may write before they have used the activities in the writing module. The "After" example is a revision of that paragraph, using the **Ten Sentence Format** and incorporating ideas from the **15 Ways to Lose the Taboos** activity and the **Reel Them In!** activity. The writing topic in the **Ten Sentence Format** example is the follow-up exercise from the **Let's Second That Emotion** activity (page 64): *Select one of the situations you identified and choose an emotion that would have better served the character as he/she strove to reach his/her goal. Explain your choice and defend it with supporting textual information.*

By using these writing activities as often as possible, teachers will note marked progress in their students' writing, as well as in their comprehension of the literature studied.

CLOSURE
—Exit Pass

The **Exit Pass** (page 45) provides the closure on a lesson. Students complete the **Exit Pass** in the last five to ten minutes of class, to show what they learned that day. The **Exit Pass** lets teachers assess whether or not students are reaching the preset goals. If they are not, the teacher can question students for clarification and can modify lessons before the next class to keep students on track. It provides another way for teachers to regularly check the foundational knowledge of all the students.

ANALYZE THIS!
Novel/Short Story Review

Name:_____ Period:_____ Date:_____

Address each of the following points with specific facts, details, and examples from the story. Your answers will show how well you know and understand what you read. On the day of the review, be sure to bring up any areas where you need clarification.

1. Who is the protagonist? The antagonist? Name and identify other important characters.

Protagonist:_____

Antagonist:_____

Other characters:_____

2. Describe the setting/locale:

_____

_____

_____

_____

3. What is the central conflict/problem that the protagonist is facing? Explain whether it is psychological, physical, emotional, spiritual, or a mixture of all of these issues.

_____

_____

_____

_____

4. Describe three ways in which the protagonist's and antagonist's personalities are revealed (actions, reactions, words, other character's words, etc).

Protagonist:_____

_____

_____

_____

Antagonist:_____

_____

_____

_____

5. Reveal the five stages of the plot:

Exposition:_____

_____

_____

_____

Rising action (one complication per line): Just give the complication, not the main character's responses. _____

_____

_____

_____

_____

_____

_____

Climax: _____

_____

_____

_____

Falling action (one event per line): _____

_____

_____

_____

_____

Resolution: _____

_____

_____

_____

6. Describe the tone/mood using a minimum of five specific adjectives or expressions:

_____

_____

_____

_____

7. Give three symbols and explain what they represent.
   A. _____
   B. _____
   C. _____

8. State the theme—the universal message that the author imparted. Explain how you derived this idea. _____

_____

_____

_____

_____

_____

ANALYZE THIS! RESULTS

Class/Period: _____ Date: _____

HP = Highly Proficent   P = Proficient   SP = Some Proficiency   NP = Not Proficient

Student Name	Character	Plot	Conflict	POV	Tone	Symbols	Theme

TEACHER NOTES
Taboo Words & Phrases

1. The first day of school, hand out the **Taboo Words & Phrases** sheet to every student. They are to refer to it every time that they revise a draft of an essay, an original poem or fiction piece, or a narrative article. Even if students revise only for these particular words and phrases, their writing will dramatically improve.

2. When students use these weak and clichéd words and phrases, their writing is vague, emotionless, and *tells* instead of *shows*. No matter what type of writing, students should strive to create word pictures; to *show*, not *tell*, and to use concrete, specific nouns and adjectives.

3. Verbs are the backbone of writing, and should always show action and the emotion of the subject performing the action.

4. Repeat this information over and over to the students and address it on their final drafts. **Taboo Words & Phrases** also works as a poster to hang in the classroom. For a poster, add the following information:

   Effective Writing:

   - Shows instead of tells

   - Creates word pictures

   - Uses concrete, specific nouns and adjectives

   - Uses strong verbs to form the writing's backbone; verbs must show action and emotion

NOTE: *As a visual activity and for reinforcement, have various students come into the room, and ask the rest of the class to choose a verb that shows not only how each person moved but also the emotion he/she expressed in his/her movements, i.e., sidled, strutted, slumped, etc.*

TABOO WORDS & PHRASES

Just say NO

to the following words and phrases in your writing:

1. *–Go, went, (have) gone, going*
   –Get, got, (have) gotten
   –Walk, walked, (have) walked
   –Look, looked, (have)looked
   –See, saw, (have) seen
   These verbs show no emotion and give weak and vague action. Say **NO** to them!

2. . . . "Has been there for me" . . . So cliché!

3. . . . Starting sentences with *it* or *there* and a *to be* verb; these are wasted words that say nothing.

4. . . . Second Person: *you* (except in dialogue); NEVER talk to the reader except to give instructions.

5. . . . Overuse of *to be* verbs (*am, is, are, was, were*) as the main verb in a sentence/phrase.

6. . . . *Thing*: Empty, empty word!

7. . . . Indefinite pronouns (*any* or *some* plus *body* or *thing*, etc.).

8. . . . Starting too many sentences with *I* and beginning any two consecutive sentences with the same word.

REMEMBER:
ONLY *YOU* CAN PREVENT DULL WRITING
THAT TELLS INSTEAD OF SHOWS!

TEACHER NOTES
15 Days to Lose the Taboos

1. Make sure students refer to the **Taboo Words & Phrases** chart while they complete the activities.

2. Have students complete one of the activities each day, using warm-ups or rough drafts of current pieces.

3. The time limit for Days 1 through 12 should be 10 to 15 minutes.

4. Allot 20 minutes for days 13 through 15.

5. The activities do not have to be finished in any specific order, but an effective start is often with the weak verbs.

6. When the lesson calls for word lists (days 1 through 5), instruct students to set aside a separate section in their notebooks for these and any other word lists they will create throughout the year. Note: students may also make 15-word lists for the five senses, for words that express various emotions (joy, sadness, anger, etc.), for colors, and many more.

7. This work can be checked in a variety of ways:
    - During the activity, teachers can walk around and check that students are on task, but have them turn in all of the revised work with the final draft of the assignment.
    - Students can keep all of the revisions in their notebooks, to turn in on an assigned day, and receive a grade separate from the essay, poem, fiction piece or article.
    - Each activity can be graded as a separate entity.

15 DAYS TO LOSE THE TABOOS

Revise warm-ups/rough drafts for the following Taboo Words & Phrases:

DAY 1: go, went, (have, has, had) gone, going

Make a list of 15 verbs that can replace this weak verb

DAY 2: get, got (have, has, had) gotten

Make a list of 15 verbs to replace this weak verb

DAY 3: walk, walked (have, has, had) walked

Make a list of 15 verbs to replace this weak verb

DAY 4: look, looked, (have has, had) looked

Make a list of 15 verbs to replace this weak verb

DAY 5: see, saw, (have, has, had) seen

Make a list of 15 verbs to replace this weak verb

DAY 5: "Has been there for me"

Make a list of 10 words to replace this horribly clichéd phrase

DAY 6: Starting sentences with *it* or *there* and a *to be* verb (*am, is, are, was, were; have, has, had*)

Rewrite 5 sentences that previously began with *it/there* and a *to be* verb

DAY 7:

Same activity as Day 6.

DAY 8:

1. Replace any usage of second person *you*, except when it is used in dialogue
2. Rewrite 10 sentences, changing from second person to first or third

DAY 9:

1. Find 10 sentences using *am, is, are, was, were* as the main verb
2. Revise those sentences, replacing them with verbs that show action and emotion

DAY 10:

Same activity as Day 9.

DAY 11:

1. Vertically number a sheet of paper from 1 to 15.
2. Using a warm-up or a rough draft of a piece, write the first word of every sentence for 15 consecutive sentences.
3. Rewrite the sentences, making sure that each one begins with a different word.

DAY 12:

1. Using warm-ups or a rough draft, find 15 times where you used the word *thing* and circle it each time.
2. Revise the sentences, replacing the word *thing* with a concrete, specific noun.

DAY 13:

1. Revise a warm-up or rough draft, replacing any of the items on the Taboo Words & Phrases.
2. Label it with today's date and the word *revised*.

DAY 14 AND 15:

The same as Day 13.

TEACHER NOTES
Reel Them In!

To reel in the reader, the writer must bait a "hook." The writing must **be specific**.
Reel Them In! has 20 exercises where students can practice writing hooks and being specific. Teachers can use them in a variety of ways:

A. For warm-ups:
Part 1: Choose an exercise, and give students 10 - 15 minutes to complete it.
Part 2: Give students 5 minutes to write a hook using their response from Part 1 (for exercises 1 - 4, they should choose one of their responses).

B. Print the list of exercises. Let students pick one, write their response, and then write a hook using that response.

C. Use these for practice every day or periodically, until you feel the students are proficient in writing hooks. They are always good to use as students finish tests and their peers are still working, or anytime there are a few minutes to fill.

For each response, let students choose the type of response (fiction, narrative non-fiction, personal essay, descriptive piece, expository essay, newspaper story, etc.) or assign the type of response they should write.

REEL THEM IN!

Good writers know that they must snag readers with the first few sentences. If they don't, chances are the piece will sink into oblivion. Think of the lead sentences as a fishing hook, and every word that forms each sentence as the bait. The hook has one main purpose: luring readers to the writer's world. Readers are more apt to keep reading if the writer grabs their attention.

TYPES OF HOOKS:

- **Anecdote**: relates an emotional or exciting part of a situation
  The longer my fingertips wrapped themselves in the scarlet and gold cashmere scarf, the more my desire for it mushroomed. I closed my eyes, visualizing my neck decorated like October's maple trees. My yearning blocked any common sense from my brain. "Just this once," I argued to myself as my hands edged the treasure toward my jacket pocket.

- **Description of person, place or object**: paints a word picture
  At eleven o'clock every day, Maude hobbled to the wooden bench in the loneliest corner of the park and slumped onto its splintery slats. After easing a wrinkled letter from its envelope, she would study it again and again as tears dripped from her faded blue eyes onto her tattered gray sweater.

- **Example**: Develops a specific instead of a general idea
  Many factors can erode teenagers' academic success. Among these are lack of sleep, extra-curricular activities, and procrastination.

- **Stance on an issue**: clarifies the writer's opinion on a controversial point
  Any high school that chooses to delay the start of school by an hour or more might as well have a funeral for interscholastic athletics.

- **Startling fact or statement**: to shock the readers
  Four out of ten adolescent girls will be the victims of dating abuse.

- **Question**: this is an acceptable format, but is a very, very weak choice. The purpose of writing is to answer the readers' questions.

CHOOSING THE RIGHT WORDS:

- **Strong concrete nouns and adjectives:** help create clear mental pictures. They destroy haziness, erase questions, and incite emotional responses. The use of sensory imagery (sight, smell, taste, touch, and hearing) lures readers. Every sentence should contain at least one sensory imagery appeal.

- **Vivid verbs:** Verbs are the backbone of writing. Without vivid verbs, writers' words will collapse. Verbs MUST combine the subject's **action** plus his/her **emotion** while performing this action.

EXAMPLES:

Weak noun:	Concrete noun:
car	Ferrari

Weak adjective:	Strong adjective:
nice	sleek

Weak verb:	Vivid verb:
drove	roared

Weak sentence:

The nice car drove into my driveway. It changed my life.

Strong sentence:

The sleek, red Ferrari roared into my driveway that golden fall afternoon, destroying my shy-girl image forever.

REEL THEM IN!
Exercises

1. Revise the following clichéd expressions to create a fresh word picture:
   - A. a goofy guy
   - B. a little pest
   - C. a beautiful sight
   - D. frozen stiff

2. Write a sentence to describe:
   - A. what you'd hear in an earthquake
   - B. what you'd smell in a bakery
   - C. how a raw onion tastes
   - D. what you'd see at a circus
   - E. what sandpaper feels like

3. Create a new simile/metaphor:
   - A. pretty as a picture
   - B. mad as a wet hen
   - C. pleased as punch
   - D. down and out
   - E. big as all outdoors

4. Write 3 sentences to establish the setting for either:
   - A. a humorous story that takes place in school, or
   - B. a sports story mystery

5. Describe the quality of light in this classroom.

6. Begin with, "I Remember." Write as many small memories as you can in the time allotted. If you get stuck, repeat the phrase, "I remember," and keep writing. Let one memory flow into another.

7. Choose a color and list as many things you can think of that you saw today in that color.

8. Describe your morning (from when you woke up until you arrived at school) as specifically as possible.

9. Take Exercise 8, describing your morning, and write about it from a third person point of view.

10. Visualize a place where you feel serene. Write about it.

11. List the people that you have loved.

12. If you were an animal, what would you be? Explain how you fit the characteristics of this animal physically and emotionally.

13. What if: Cinderella didn't live happily ever after?

14. What if: Sleeping Beauty didn't eat the poisoned apple?

15. What if: a troll lived under a nearby bridge?

16. Describe a candy bar you have invented. Draw a picture of the wrapper.

17. If you could meet a fictional character, who would it be? Why?

18. Draw the floor plan of the first house where you remember living.

19. You are sitting in Starbucks, and Bugs Bunny sits down beside you. Write your conversation.

20. Define either pain, joy, jealousy, or sadness following the pattern below: (use at least 4 of the 5 senses)

> *Loneliness is gray.*
> *It sounds like a ringing vacuum.*
> *It smells like mothballs.*
> *It tastes like sawdust.*
> *Loneliness feels like cold, wet rain soaking my cheeks.*

TEACHER NOTES
Ten Sentence Format

Bloom's Taxonomy

- Remember/Understand: describe, discuss, explain, identify
- Apply: compose
- Analyze: infer, differentiate, examine, distinguish
- Evaluate: discuss, select, give your opinion, justify
- Create: hypothesize, imagine, compose

Common Core Standards

College and Career Readiness Anchor Standards, grades 6-9

Writing: WI, W2, W3, W4, W5, W9, WIO

Language: LI, L2, L3, L6

What: **Writing About Literature**

When: Use this along with any literature study—Short stories, novels, or narrative non-fiction

Why: The **Ten Sentence Format** activity is a basic building block for students as they practice formal writing skills. Before they can write organized and coherent essays, they need to master writing the basic parts of a paragraph: the introduction (the hook, the overview or introductory statement, and the thesis statement), the body (three main ideas, each with a supporting detail), and a conclusion.

How:

- Assign this activity as an in-class exercise for a warm-up or anytime in class when you want to check students' comprehension and writing skills. Are they able to write about what they read succinctly and coherently, yet with specific details?

- Allot 20 to 30 minutes for students to complete, depending on students' skills.

- Use this activity to assess students' comprehension skills as well as their understanding of paragraph format and structure.

- Optional—after teachers assess the students' writing, they can:

  1. Reinforce the elements of a paragraph through individual or group critique lessons where students exhibit clearer understanding in their revisions (addressing Speaking & Listening Standards), and/or

  2. Have students turn the paragraph into a full-length essay

TEN SENTENCE FORMAT

25 Point total (point value for each sentence in parentheses)

Situation: _____

Hook: _____

_____

_____ (1)

Overview Statement: _____

_____ (1)

Thesis statement: _____

_____ (3)

Main Idea 1: _____

_____

_____ (3)

Supporting Detail #1 w/example: _____

_____

_____ (2)

Main Idea 2: _____

_____

_____ (3)

Supporting Detail #2 w/example: _____

_____

_____ (2)

Main Idea 3: _____

_____

_____ (3)

Supporting Detail #3 w/example: _____

_____

_____ (2)

Concluding Statement: _____

_____

_____ (5)

TEN SENTENCE FORMAT
From *Animal Farm* by George Orwell

ACTIVITY (from **Let's Second that Emotion!**):

Select one of the situations you identified and choose an emotion that would have better served the character as he/she strove to reach his/her goal. Explain your choice and defend it with supporting textual information.

BEFORE LEARNING THE TEN SENTENCE FORMAT:

Snowball thought that the windmill would make less work for the animals. He might have been smart enough to think up this idea and make great speeches, but he was stupid to trust Napoleon the bully. Bullies will never put up with anyone who has ideas that might push them out of power. When Snowball spread out his plans during a town meeting and tried to explain them, Napoleon peed on them. Then Napoleon had the dogs chase Snowball off of the farm. It was dumb of Snowball to trust him and think that Napoleon would be there for him because they were the power pigs. If Snowball had been more street-wise about his rival, he would have let Napoleon take credit for the idea and he would still be on the farm.

TEN SENTENCE FORMAT

Situation: Select one of the situations you identified and choose an emotion that would have better served the character as he/she strove to reach his/her goal. Explain your choice and defend it with supporting textual information.

Hook: If Snowball had been sharp enough to understand the saying, "Keep your friends close and your enemies closer," he might have remained the idea pig in "Animal Farm" by George Orwell. _____ (1)

Overview Statement: Snowball's plan for the windmill stayed true to the beliefs of Animalism because it would have cut down on the animals' work. _____ (1)

Thesis statement: If he had thought about his past disagreements with Napoleon on other farming issues, Snowball would have realized that his brains needed a dose of deceit if he were to match Napoleon's brawn in their struggle for power. _____ (3)

Main Idea 1: Snowball naively believed that his brilliant speeches would win him fan support. _____ (3)

Supporting Detail #1 w/example: The modern farming ideas that he had read about in Mr. Jones's magazines excited Snowball, but he loved his windmill plan since it would bring electricity to the farm and a three-day workweek to the animals. _____ (2)

Main Idea 2: Napoleon's sneaky dealings were far more powerful. _____ (3)

Supporting Detail #2 w/example: He encouraged the sheep to interrupt Snowball's speeches by bleating, "Four legs good, two legs bad," and trained the dogs to attack his rival on his command. _____ (2)

Main Idea 3: The town meeting about the windmill proved to be the showdown between these two adversaries. _____ (3)

Supporting Detail #3 w/example: When Snowball tried to present his windmill plans, the sheep caused a disturbance with their bleating, Napoleon urinated on the designs and then ordered the snarling dogs to chase Snowball from the farm forever. _____ (2)

Concluding Statement: Snowball's gullibility about Napoleon's desire to be the top pig led to his defeat because he never understood that the lust for power will destroy alliances. _____ (5)

TEACHER NOTES
Exit Pass

Print multiple copies of the **Exit Pass** page and cut them into individual exit passes.

Begin this activity ten minutes before the end of the period. Allow the first five minutes for students to complete it. For the last five minutes, allow students to talk about any specific problems understanding or completing that day's work.

If teachers wish, they may use it as a daily grade. Example: Each **Exit Pass** is worth 1 point per day.

Teachers should review the Exit Passes before the next class and take notes on what worked and what didn't so they can tweak their lessons to meet student needs if necessary.

EXIT PASS

Name:_____ Period:_____ Date:_____

Three ideas, concepts, thoughts I learned today are:

I. _____
   _____

2. _____
   _____

3. _____
   _____

EXIT PASS

Name:_____ Period:_____ Date:_____

Three ideas, concepts, thoughts I learned today are:

I. _____
   _____

2. _____
   _____

3. _____
   _____

EXIT PASS

Name:_____ Period:_____ Date:_____

Three ideas, concepts, thoughts I learned today are:

I. _____
   _____

2. _____
   _____

3. _____
   _____

CHAPTER 3

THE FRAMEWORK

The blueprint for this program has been drawn, and the foundation has been cemented into place. Now it is time to build the framework—helping students understand how each element of literature is integral to the whole piece. No element can stand alone. Each one depends on the others to give meaning, complexity, and a reason for existing.

John Dunne said, "No man is an island, entire of itself. Each is a piece of the continent, a part of the main." The same can be said for each element of literature. These elements should never be taught as a list of literary terms, but rather, always presented in conjunction with some type of literature: a short story, a novel, or narrative nonfiction.

The activities included in this book are organized into modules based on the elements of literature. Teachers can choose among the many activities offered to teach new concepts and to reinforce students' knowledge. These activities run the gamut from basic to complex. Each one requires students to use various inductive and deductive reasoning and thinking skills to process the information, to question literal and figurative elements, and to think analytically, creatively, and logically.

Teacher Notes introduce each activity. These help guide teachers as they use the activities with their students. Teacher Notes include:

Common Core Standards

Grades 6 through 9. Grade-specific standards require students to show stronger and more thorough textual evidence and deeper understanding of the material under study.

Bloom's Taxonomy

Verbs from the middle level of Bloom's Taxonomy are suggested, for teachers who use this paradigm. Teachers can see how the Common Core Standards and Bloom's Taxonomy link together.

WHAT element of literature is being explored

Each activity helps teach concepts about specific elements of literature, i.e., character, plot, theme, etc.

WHEN the activity should be introduced

At what time during the study of the literature should this activity be used? Timing is suggested—i.e., before starting the reading, after the rising action but before the climax, etc.

WHY the activity is important

The Teacher Notes for each activity specify exactly what the students will learn

HOW the activity should be used

The procedure for the teacher to follow is outlined in detail for each activity, including preparation, time mangement during the activity, and follow-up suggestions.

For each activity, teachers must also consider WHO they are teaching. Use the information from the Unit Structure Chart (p. 20) to specify grade level, student needs, and learning styles.

These activities can be used over and over throughout the year with any literature and nonfiction the students are reading. The modules are flexible. Teachers can use some of the activities or all of them, depending on student skills and learning levels. They can be used with all learners, from those with rudimentary knowledge, comprehension, and writing skills to those with advanced skills.

By learning how the elements of literature mesh to create a strong framework in literature, students will build solid houses of comprehension that can't be blown down by any Big Bad Wolf!

MODULES

Pre-Reading Comprehension
- What Do I Know? How Do I Know It?
- Aha! So This Is What It's About

Analyzing Character
- Time For Body Building
- Fact or Opinion? You Be the Judge
- Let's Second That Emotion
- Why Did You Do That?
- What's My Line: Protagonist or Antagonist?

Analyzing Conflict/Plot
- Plotting Along
- It's Complicated
- What's the Conflict?
- It Is the Cause
- Conflict Connections
- Gender Issues

Analyzing Setting
- What Kind of World Does the Author Create?
- Setting it Up

General Reading Comprehension
- Green Light! Red Light!
- Journals: Response Letters
- What Was I Thinking?
- Author, Author, What's Your Purpose?

TEACHER NOTES
What Do I Know? How Do I Know It?

Common Core Standards

College and Career Readiness Anchor Standards, grades 6-9

Reading: RI

Writing: WI, W10

Speaking & Listening: SLI

Language: LI, L2

Bloom's Taxonomy

- Remember/Understand: restate, paraphrase, give examples
- Apply: organize, generalize, choose
- Analyze: infer, select, point out, analyze
- Evaluate: consider, summarize, conclude, compare
- Create: suggest, rearrange, create

What: **Pre-reading Comprehension**

When: Prior to students reading the text

Why: Before students begin to read the assigned material, they need to evaluate the general design of the text. This activity has students combine the story's general information regarding character, plot, and conflict with their prior knowledge of these elements of literature. They also link the people and events in the story to their own lives and knowledge of the world.

How:

- Introduce the textual material.
- Hand out books; if using an anthology, direct students to the assigned pages. For a book, students should read the first five pages; for a short story, students should read the first two pages.
- Hand out the **What Do I Know? How Do I Know It?** exercise. Review directions.
- Allot 10-15 minutes for Part 1. The time allotted will depend on the students' reading abilities. Allow for more time if needed.
- Divide students into groups of three, mixing the students' ability levels.
- Allot 10 minutes for Part 2. The time allotted will depend on the students' reading abilities. Allow for more time if needed.
- Lead a whole-class discussion, with each student trio explaining their choices in Part 2.

MORE ⟹

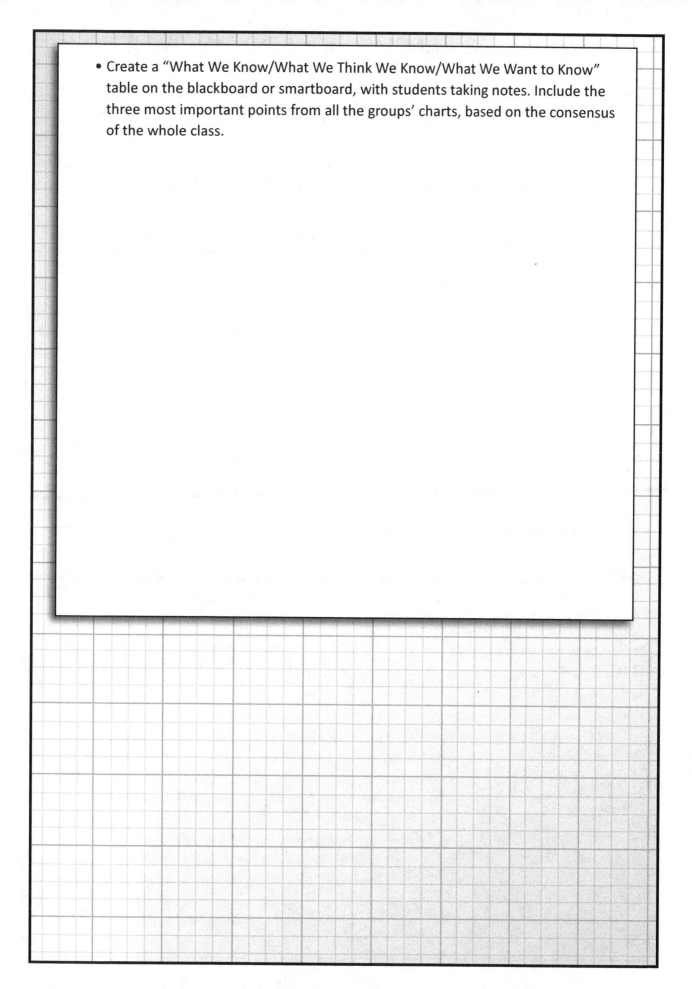

- Create a "What We Know/What We Think We Know/What We Want to Know" table on the blackboard or smartboard, with students taking notes. Include the three most important points from all the groups' charts, based on the consensus of the whole class.

WHAT DO I KNOW? HOW DO I KNOW IT?

Name:_____ Period:_____ Date:_____

Text:_____ Author:_____

PART 1: Individually, read the back and inside covers of the book (if provided), and the first five pages. When you have finished, fill out the following chart individually.

What We Know	What We Think We Know	What We Want to Know

PART 2: After you have completed Part 1, discuss what you wrote with the rest of your teacher-assigned trio and then reach a consensus on three points for each of the following and complete the following chart as a group.

What We Know	What We Think We Know	What We Want to Know

TEACHER NOTES
Aha! So *This* Is What It's About!

Bloom's Taxonomy

- Remember/Understand: summarize, give examples, identify

- Apply: choose, show

- Analyze: analyze, infer, differentiate

- Evaluate: conclude, give an opinion, justify

- Create: hypothesize, imagine

Common Core Standards

College and Career Readiness Anchor Standards, grades 6-9

Reading: RI, R2, R4

Writing: WI, WIO

Speaking & Listening: SLI, SL2

Language: LI, L2, L3

What: **Pre-reading Comprehension**

When: Students complete this activity after they have read the assigned number of pages at the start of the text. Teachers should be sure to assign enough of the text to provide students with sufficient specific character, plot, and setting details so they can complete this activity.

Why: Students need to understand the basic components of character, plot, and setting, and how they work together to create a strong story structure. These elements work as the vehicle to enable students to differentiate between factual and opinion-based material, a crucial reading strategy needed for optimal comprehension.

How:

- Lead the students in a discussion: What constitutes a fact? What constitutes an opinion? Write these working definitions on the board.

- Assign reading length: For a book, students should read the first 10 pages; for a short story, students should read the first half of the story.

- Allot 15 minutes for students to individually complete both Parts 1 and 2 of the activity. The aim is to assess general student understanding of the text with regard to character, setting, plot/conflict, and mood. They should not embellish their answers with depth and details at this point.

MORE ⟹

- Create a chart on the board as below, leaving enough space for each student to add a detail under *Fact* or *Opinion:*

	Fact	Opinion
Protagonist	_____	_____
Antagonist	_____	_____
Supporting Characters	_____	_____
Setting	_____	_____
Conflict	_____	_____
Mood	_____	_____

- Have each student add a fact (Part 1) or opinion (Part 2) to the chart on the board and include his/her initials. Have students explain how they decided if their point was a fact or an opinion.

- Lead a whole-class discussion to amend the previous definitions of fact and opinion. Instruct students to write them on the back of the activity sheet for future reference (Example: a fact can be proven—a truth; an opinion can't be proven—a matter of personal judgment and insufficient evidence).

- Closure: Students complete an Exit Pass (page 45).

AHA! SO THIS IS WHAT IT'S ABOUT

Name:_____ Period:_____ Date:_____

Novel:_____ Author:_____

Part 1: And that's a fact!

Read the first 10 pages of the book or the first half of the short story. Then summarize the facts about the following topics: characters (give their names), setting, conflict (who and what), and mood.

Protagonist _____
_____
_____

Antagonist _____
_____
_____

Supporting Characters
_____
_____
_____
_____

Setting _____
_____

Conflict _____
_____

Mood (Choose specific references to support your choice)_____
_____

Part 2: This is my opinion . . .

Make inferences about the characters and their relationships, as well as what you think will happen, and hypothesize about the events that you think will occur. Give details to support your thoughts.

Characters and their relationships _____
_____

Action and Events _____
_____
_____

TEACHER NOTES
Time for Body Building

Bloom's Taxonomy

- Remember/Understand: describe, explain, identify
- Apply: compose
- Analyze: infer, differentiate, examine, determine
- Evaluate: conclude, discuss, verify, support
- Create: hypothesize, imagine, compose

Common Core Standards

College and Career Readiness Anchor Standards, grades 6-9

Reading: R1, R3

Writing: W1, W2, W10

Speaking & Listening: SL4

Language: L1, L2, L3, L6

What: **Character Development**. Students will strengthen their inductive and deductive reasoning skills.

When: Use throughout the study of any text. Keep a stack of sheets on hand so students can pick up more when needed.

Why: Character development is one of the most important and most basic elements of literature. This activity helps teachers discuss all aspects of character development, including: how the author develops characters, character styles (flat/static; round/dynamic), and direct and indirect characterization. For maximum comprehension, students must be active, not passive, participants. They must not only decode the text, but must be able to think about and apply emotions, experience, and knowledge from their personal lives to the characters.

How:

- Give each student one sheet for the protagonist, one for the antagonist, and one for each character they plan to include in the study. Students can get more sheets as needed. Each student should get a packet the day the literature is introduced and keep these throughout their study of the book.

- Lead a whole-class discussion reviewing the characteristics of a protagonist and an antagonist.

- Students should add to these sheets after each reading segment is completed.

MORE ⟹

- Students do not have to copy the complete citations, just the words and phrases that show aspects of each character. Remind them to include page numbers.
- Students should refer to their notes during class discussions on character.
- Teacher can check for additional details each day as they walk through the class. Doing this during warm-up time works well.

FOLLOW-UP EXERCISE *Your job is to introduce one of the characters at an assembly. Use the information you have gathered about the character. Write your introduction in 200 words or less.*

GRADING SUGGESTION *Students can receive a grade for each sheet turned in daily, or receive a grade for complete note packets turned in on a specified day. A separate grade should be given for the follow-up exercise.*

TIME FOR BODY BUILDING

Name:_____ Period:_____ Date:_____

Flesh out each character by writing notes/phrases from the story that show the following information about the characters. Be sure to include page numbers. Use a separate sheet for the protagonist, the antagonist and any other major player

Character _____ Book _____

What the character thinks about him/herself:

_____
_____
_____
_____
_____
_____
_____

What the character says about him/herself:

_____
_____
_____
_____
_____
_____
_____

What others think/say about the character:

_____
_____
_____
_____
_____
_____
_____

What the author thinks/says about the character:

_____
_____
_____
_____
_____
_____
_____

TEACHER NOTES
Fact or Opinion? You Be the Judge

Bloom's Taxonomy

- Remember/Understand: describe, expand, explain, identify
- Apply: construct, record, compose
- Analyze: infer, differentiate, distinguish, determine
- Evaluate: discuss, conclude, give your opinion, justify
- Create: imagine, hypothesize, compose, produce

Common Core Standards

College and Career Readiness Anchor Standards, grades 6-9

Reading: RI, R2

Writing: WI, W2, WIO

Speaking & Listening: SLI, SL2, SL4

Language: LI, L2, L3, L4, L6

What: **Character Development**. Using the four different ways authors show character (see **Time for Body Building** activity, p. **58**), students work in groups to take this material to a more complex level. Now that they have examples about the characters in their notes, they are to discuss which are factual and which are opinions.

When: This activity can be introduced any time near the end of the rising action through the falling action.

Why: Students learn to fully flesh out the characters, as well as to differentiate between fact and opinion, which helps develop higher-level thinking skills.

How:

- Divide students into groups of three to four, depending on the class's number.

- Assign each group a different character to analyze. If any characters need to be assigned to more than one group, the protagonist and antagonist should be used more than once.

- Allot students 15 to 20 minutes to complete their charts, using their notes from the **Time for Body Building** activity. Students can use the back of the sheet for notes, if needed.

- The two "Group's Choice" squares should be issues that greatly impact the character, plot, and conflict.

- The concluding statement should be composed with input from each group member.

- When the charts are completed, each group member presents one of the categories, defending the group's fact or opinion designations.

MORE ⇨

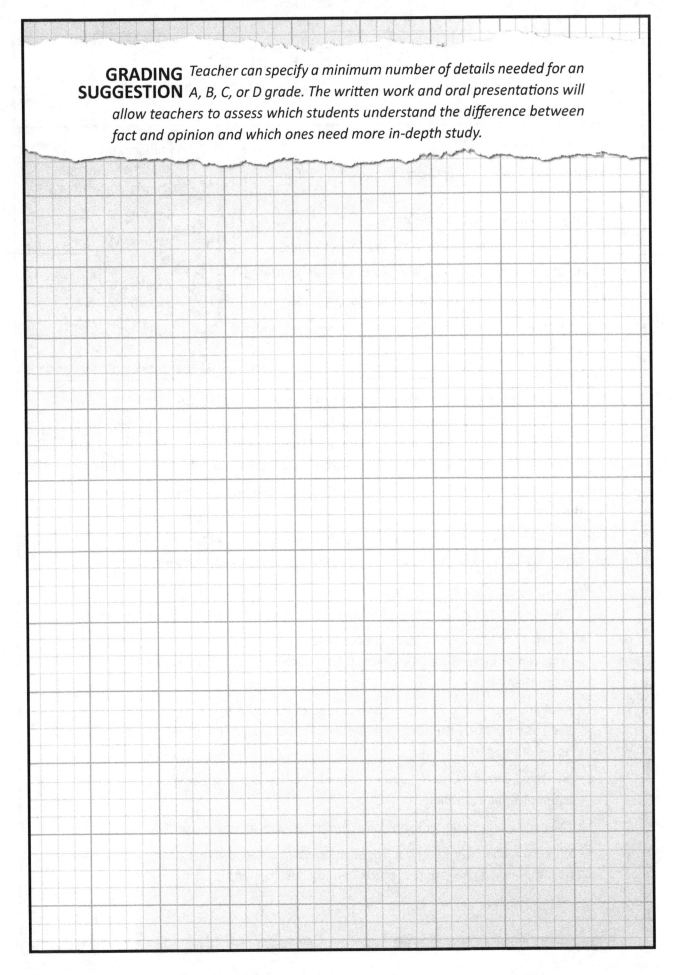

FACT OR OPINION? YOU BE THE JUDGE

Name:_____ Period:_____ Date:_____

In groups, analyze your assigned character by writing everything you know about that person: appearance, personality, beliefs, friends, enemies, conflicts, his/her driving wish, and anything else you want to include. Use a different color of crayon, pencil, or marker for each category. Organize the chart in any way your group chooses. Beside each word, phrase or statement, write an **F** if it is a fact and **O** if it is an opinion. Make the chart visually pleasing. The concluding statement should be focused, strong, and reveal a clear word picture about the character.

Character _____

Appearance	Personality	Beliefs
Friends	Enemies	Conflict
Driving Wish	Group's Choice	Group's Choice

Concluding Statement_____
_____
_____
_____
_____
_____

TEACHER NOTES
Let's Second That Emotion!

Bloom's Taxonomy

- Remember/Understand: name, explain, identify
- Apply: compose
- Analyze: infer, differentiate, examine, deduce
- Evaluate: conclude, support, decide, evaluate
- Create: hypothesize, imagine, compose

Common Core Standards

College and Career Readiness Anchor Standards, grades 6-9

Reading: RI, R3

Writing: WI, W2, WIO

Speaking & Listening: SLI, SL2, SL3, SL4

Language: LI, L2, L3, L4, L6

What: **Character Development**. Students must use analytic thinking as well as inductive and deductive reasoning skills to show the primary motivation for a main character.

When: Use during the rising action of the story and again during the resolution to ascertain if the characters changed the emotion that drove them through the climax and falling action.

Why: This activity helps students understand the importance of how motivation, provoked by emotion, drives the plot/conflict and embellishes the story's structure. Students strengthen their comprehension skills by using various strategies such as decoding, questioning, reflecting, and applying information gleaned from their reading.

How:

- On the board, write entertainment categories such as: *Novels, Short Stories, Poems (or Song Lyrics), Movies,* and *Television Shows.*

- Lead a whole-class discussion about how emotions drive protagonists and antagonists to act and react to situations.

- Divide the class up in equal groups and assign one category to each group. Each student individually prepares an example from his/her category that includes: the title of the book, movie, etc., the character's name, a *P* for protagonist and an *A* for antagonist, and the emotion that drives that person's

MORE ⟹

motivation. The teacher calls each student to the board to add his/her information to the class chart (sample on page 66), continuing in this manner until all students have participated in the board work.

- After the discussion, hand out **Let's Second That Emotion** and review the directions with the students. Each student completes the activity sheet individually.

- Allot 15 to 20 minutes to complete the activity.

- To conclude the lesson, ask several students to read their choices for the situations, the accompanying emotion, and their explanatory example.

FOLLOW-UP EXERCISE *Have students select one of the situations he/she identified and choose an emotion that would have better served the character as the character strove to reach his/her goal. Students should explain their choice and defend it with supporting textual information. (This can be assigned as homework, with various students sharing their responses at the next class meeting.)*

CLASS CHART - LET'S SECOND THAT EMOTION

Novel

Title	Character	P/A	Emotion

Short Story

Title	Character	P/A	Emotion

Poem/Song Lyrics

Title	Character	P/A	Emotion

Movie

Title	Character	P/A	Emotion

TV Shows

Title	Character	P/A	Emotion

LET'S SECOND THAT EMOTION!
(Individual Student Chart)

Name:_____ Period:_____ Date:_____

Love, curiosity, self-preservation, greed, self-discovery, duty, honor, revenge—What emotion motivates the protagonist or antagonist in the book you are reading?

- Explore the motivations of the protagonist, the antagonist, and three characters of your choice. Write each character's name in the left-hand column. Label the protagonist with a **P** and the antagonist with an **A**.

- In the middle column, select a situation involving this person.

- In the right-hand column, identify the primary emotion that motivates that character's actions/reactions.

- Explain your choice with a specific example from the book in the space under *Example*.

Character	Situation	Emotion
1.		
Example:		
2.		
Example:		
3.		
Example:		
4.		
Example:		
5.		
Example:		

TEACHER NOTES
Why Did You Do *That?*

Bloom's Taxonomy

- Remember/Understand: name, explain, identify, describe

- Apply: compose

- Analyze: infer, differentiate, examine, distinguish

- Evaluate: conclude, support, decide, evaluate, select

- Create: hypothesize, imagine, suggest, suppose, compose

Common Core Standards

College and Career Readiness Anchor Standards, grades 6-9

Reading: RI, R3

Writing: WI, W2, WIO

Speaking & Listening: SL2. SL3, SL4

Language: LI, L2, L3, L4, L6

What: **Character Development**. Students delve deeper into the complexities that make up a character.

When: Assign this activity during the rising action of the book, because these are the parts of the story where the characters' actions and reactions to a situation are crucial to the climax. Use the activity at a point when students have enough textual information about the character to support their analyses.

Why: Students are required to utilize all of their reading strategies: decoding, summarizing, questioning, clarifying, reflecting, and applying. This assignment will show teachers which students clearly comprehend the causes and effects of the character's decisions and those who need more help in understanding, evaluating, and decoding character.

How:

- Hand out the activity and review the directions.

- Allot students 20 minutes to complete this activity, reminding them that their answers must show specific textual support in the note boxes.

- When the time is up, call on various students, each with a different character, to read their answers.

- End this segment of the class with students choosing three peer solutions that they feel would have been better choices for the character. Write these on the board. Students can copy them on the back of the activity sheet.

WHY DID YOU DO *THAT?*

Name:_____ Period:_____ Date:_____

Choose a character in the book and summarize how he/she handled a situation. Next, discuss how you would have liked the character to have resolved the situation. Finally, be sure to address the following points: *How would the character have to change to handle the event this way? How would these changes affect the book's resolution?* Use the boxes to take notes before writing your explanations.

```
                        ┌─────────────────┐
                        │    Situation    │
                        │                 │
                        │                 │
                        │                 │
                        └────────┬────────┘
        ┌────────────────────────┼────────────────────────┐
┌───────┴────────┐      ┌────────┴────────┐      ┌─────────┴───────┐
│  Your solution │      │ Character changes│      │   Resolution    │
│                │      │                 │      │                 │
│                │      │                 │      │                 │
│                │      │                 │      │                 │
└────────────────┘      └─────────────────┘      └─────────────────┘
```

Situation Analysis (What the character did and why):

_____

_____

_____

Your Solution:

_____

_____

_____

How the character would have to change:

_____

_____

_____

How the new solution would affect the resolution:

_____

_____

_____

TEACHER NOTES
What's My Line: Protagonist or Antagonist?

Bloom's Taxonomy

- Remember/Understand: name, explain, identify, describe

- Apply: compose

- Analyze: infer, differentiate, examine, distinguish, determine, deduce

- Evaluate: conclude, support, decide, evaluate, select

- Create: hypothesize, imagine, suggest, suppose, compose

Common Core Standards

College and Career Readiness Anchor Standards, grades 6-9

Reading: RI, R3

Writing: WI, W2, W4, W10

Speaking & Listening: SLI, SL2, SL3, SL4

Language: LI, L2, L3, L4, L6

What: **Character Development**. Students will show their depth of understanding of characterization and what creates its complexity.

When: May be assigned at any point between the rising action and the resolution. It works best later in the story, i.e. during the falling action, as the protagonist and antagonist have had plenty of time to show their personalities and illustrate why they are the protagonist or antagonist.

Why: Requires students to show understanding of the two major types of characters in a story, and compels them to exhibit a comprehensive understanding of character. When they are finished, students should see the crucial interplay between character, conflict, and plot.

How:

- Allot 20 minutes for students to complete the activity.

- When the time is up, have the class come together for a discussion.

- Call on 5 or 6 students to read their charts.

- Tell the students not reading their papers that during the discussion they are expected to agree with or refute their peers' information and to give textual information to defend their answers.

- Require students to take notes during the discussion, especially on points where they disagree with their peers' choices and responses. They will use these notes for Part 3.

MORE ⇨

FOLLOW-UP EXERCISE *For homework, have students write a paragraph on a peer's evaluation of the protagonist or antagonist with which they disagree. Their thesis statement must say why they disagree with that choice (or the reasons for that choice). They must defend their rebuttal with textual evidence.*

WHAT'S MY LINE: PROTAGONIST OR ANTAGONIST?

Name:_____ Period:_____ Date:_____

Part I

Describe the protagonist and the antagonist in the story that you are reading by filling in the chart below with textual examples revealing information about the characters that justifies your opinion. Required information is starred. Other selections should be specific enough to paint a word picture of the character. Be prepared to defend your choices during a class discussion.

1. Physical descriptions

*2. Psychological or emotional aspects

3. What the character says about him/herself

4. What others say about the character

5. What the author says about the character

*6. Adjectives used to show the character's role

7. How the character acts and reacts to various situations

*8. The character's part in the main conflict

*9. Include one direct quote for each character where that person shows his/her role

Protagonist	Antagonist

Part 2

Show your understanding of the role of the protagonist and the antagonist in a story by listing three pieces of evidence for each role that convinced you of your choices.

Protagonist	Antagonist

Part 3: Homework

Consider your peers' choices for Protagonist and Antagonist. Review your notes from the discussion and choose one with which you disagree. Write a paragraph where you state your disagreement and defend your answer with textual evidence.

_____

_____

_____

_____

_____

_____

_____

_____

_____

_____

_____

_____

_____

_____

_____

_____

_____

_____

TEACHER NOTES
Plotting Along

Bloom's Taxonomy

- Remember/Understand: name, explain, identify, describe

- Analyze: differentiate, examine, distinguish, determine, deduce

- Evaluate: conclude, support, decide, evaluate, select

Common Core Standards

College and Career Readiness Anchor Standards, grades 6-9

Reading: R1, R3

Language: L1, L2

Speaking & Listening: SL1, SL4

What: **Plot Analysis**. Students show their understanding of the plot structure of the text.

When: Hand out this chart at the beginning of the literature study and require students to add to the sections after each reading segment.

Why: For students to understand how the plot intertwines with the other elements of literature to form a solid story structure, they need to first show their understanding of the plot components. The discussions that arise from the students' selections are perfect opportunities for teachers to assess which students truly understand plot structure and how it impacts their comprehension of the text and which ones need more clarification.

How:

- Distribute both pages of this activity (the **Plotting Along** information page and the exercise) immediately after students complete any pre-reading assignment(s).

- Review the directions with the students, stressing that students should be specific and include only those situations that are necessary for the next event to occur, and which directly lead to the climax.

- Students should add to the chart after each reading session.

- Following each reading session, call on students to read what they have added to their charts. Call on different students each day to insure that all learners participate.

- When students' choices for the rising action, climax, and falling action differ, use this discussion to clarify the criteria for the parts of the plot structure.

MORE ⇨

TRY THIS *Use additional copies of **Plotting Along** for individual reinforcement by having students choose a movie and fill in the chart. This could also be accomplished in small groups (each group picks a movie to chart) so the struggling readers can understand how and why others in their group made their decisions.*

PLOTTING ALONG

The overriding thoughts behind every plot are:
- **What do the protagonist and antagonist each want?**
- **Why is this important to each of them?**

The **EXPOSITION** (background):
- **provides basic information that the author will develop as the story unfolds**

The **INCITING MOMENT**:
- **hooks the protagonist and antagonist**
- **propels them from the rising action through to the resolution**

In the **RISING ACTION**, each complication:
- **deepens the protagonist's struggle with the antagonist**
- **stems from the one before it and leads into the next situation**

The **CLIMAX** is decision time for the protagonist, and is:
- **the point where all of the tension reaches a boil**
- **the point when the reader knows whether or not the protagonist achieves his/her goal**

The **FALLING ACTION**:
- **clarifies the events that occur after the climax**

The **DENOUEMENT**:
- **ties together any loose ends from the plot, the subplots and the characters**

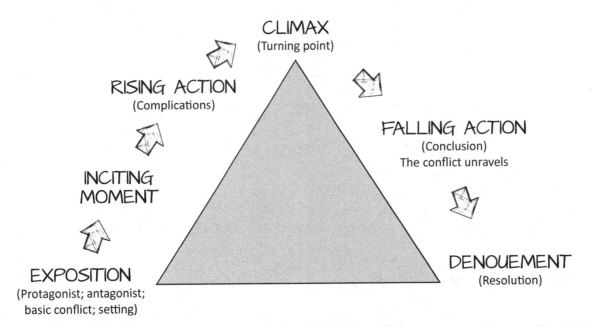

CLIMAX
(Turning point)

RISING ACTION
(Complications)

FALLING ACTION
(Conclusion)
The conflict unravels

INCITING
MOMENT

EXPOSITION
(Protagonist; antagonist;
basic conflict; setting)

DENOUEMENT
(Resolution)

PLOTTING ALONG

Name:_____ Period:_____ Date:_____

Refer to the **Plotting Along** information page for details about each section of the Plot Diagram. For each section of the plot, write the specific events that happen in that section. BE SPECIFIC! Be sure to include only those situations that are necessary for the next event to occur, and which directly lead to the climax. The author provides some information solely for the purpose of developing the setting, characters, tone, symbols and theme. These are not necessarily included on a Plot Diagram.

Note: The numbers are just a suggestion. You might need fewer or more; this depends on the length and depth of the text.

Exposition:

1. _____
2. _____
3. _____

Inciting Moment:_____
_____

Rising Action:

1. _____
2. _____
3. _____
4. _____
5. _____
6. _____
7. _____
8. _____
9. _____
10. _____

Climax:_____
_____

Falling Action:

1. _____
2. _____
3. _____
4. _____

Denouement:_____
_____

TEACHER NOTES
It's Complicated

Bloom's Taxonomy

- Remember/Understand: name, explain, identify, describe

- Apply: compose

- Analyze: infer, differentiate, examine, distinguish, determine, deduce

- Evaluate: evaluate, select, give your opinion, defend

- Create: hypothesize, imagine, suppose, compose

Common Core Standards

College and Career Readiness Anchor Standards, grades 6-9

Reading: RI, R3

Writing: WI, W2, WIO

Speaking & Listening: SLI, SL4

Language: LI, L2, L3

What: Plot Analysis. This activity has students focus on the protagonist's main goal, the complications that impact his/her quest to achieve this dream, and the character's actions and reactions.

When: In conjunction with the **Plotting Along** activity.

Why: In **Plotting Along,** students are asked to give only factual information. Using the **It's Complicated** activity, students strengthen their comprehension levels by utilizing higher-order thinking and reasoning skills to interpret the text, reflect on the character's emotions that lead to his/her actions, and apply their knowledge.

How:

- Use this activity as a warm-up exercise following each reading session or as a writing break during the class discussions on plot.

- Students can add to their responses as the discussion of the text progresses.

TRY THIS *Since the discussion of plot will always include the characters, teachers can have students refer to **Let's Second That Emotion!** (page 64) and/or **Why Did You Do That?** (page 68) to reinforce the fact that all the components of the elements of literature work together to create a strong story structure.*

IT'S COMPLICATED

Name:_____ Period:_____ Date:_____

Every story, whether 6 pages or 600, revolves around one premise: What does the main character want? This desire must be of utmost importance to the protagonist. He or she must be ready to do whatever it takes to attain this objective. State the main character's key intention. Then, list the complications and setbacks he/she encounters and show his/her response to each one. Finally, discuss the final outcome.

Character:_____ Book:_____ Author:_____

Character's Main Objective:_____

_____

Complication:_____

_____

Character's Action/Reaction: _____

_____

_____

Complication:_____

_____

Character's Action/Reaction: _____

_____

_____

Complication:_____

_____

Character's Action/Reaction: _____

_____

_____

Complication:_____

_____

Character's Action/Reaction: _____

_____

_____

Climax (Turning Point):_____

_____

Resolution: Evaluate the character's actions and state whether he/she was worthy of realizing his/her dream.

_____

_____

_____

_____

_____

_____

TEACHER NOTES
What's the Conflict?

Bloom's Taxonomy

- Remember/Understand: name, explain, identify, describe

- Apply: compose

- Analyze: differentiate, examine, determine, categorize

- Evaluate: conclude, decide, debate, justify

- Create: hypothesize, imagine, suggest, compose

Common Core Standards

College and Career Readiness Anchor Standards, grades 6-9

Reading: RI, R3, R10

Writing: WI, W2, W4, WIO

Speaking & Listening: SLI, SL2, SL3, SL4

Language: LI, L2, L3, L4, L6

What: **Plot Analysis.** This activity examines the connections between characters and their motivations, plot, and conflict.

When: This activity can be used as the plot unfolds, but the types of conflict are easier to interpret and analyze during the resolution of the story, since the characters, their motivations, and the plot have been fully developed then.

Why: Students understand the separate entities of character, character motivation, plot, and conflict, but also comprehend how they rely on each other to keep the story structure from collapsing. As each of the elements becomes more and more interconnected, students utilize their ability to process the textual information, to ask questions when they need clarity, and to exercise their creative and analytical thinking skills.

How:

- Hand out the activity and have students work individually for 15 minutes.

- Divide the students into groups of three to share their answers and evidence. As they debate and defend their answers, students can choose to keep their choices and reasoning or revise their answers.

- While they are working, teacher should write each of the types of conflict across the black/whiteboard.

- Five students at a time come to the board and write their names under the conflict(s) they selected that impacted the protagonist's life the most.

MORE⇨

- As each student sits down, teacher brings up another student to add his/her name under a conflict on the board until all students have responded. During the ensuing discussion, students should justify their choices with evidence from the story.

- If any conflict types are not chosen, and the teacher agrees with the students' choices, those conflicts should be erased. If the teacher doesn't agree, he/she can lead the students in discussion using open-ended questions.

- Two or three students can read their "Tell Us About It" paragraphs to conclude the lesson.

WHAT'S THE CONFLICT?
People + Personal Motivation = Conflict

Name:_____ Period:_____ Date:_____

Choose which conflict(s) impact the protagonist's life the most. Give three pieces of evidence that support the choice. Write N/A In the evidence space if this conflict does NOT occur in the story.

Main Character (Protagonist): _____

Conflict	Evidence
CHARACTER VS. CHARACTER	
CHARACTER VS. SOCIETY	
CHARACTER VS. SELF	
CHARACTER VS. NATURE	
CHARACTER VS. MACHINE	
CHARACTER VS. SUPERNATURAL	

Tell us about it: On the back of this paper, distinguish which of the six conflicts impacted the character the most physically, emotionally, spiritually, and morally. Justify your choice with information from the story.

TEACHER NOTES
It Is the Cause

Bloom's Taxonomy

- Remember/Understand: name, explain, identify, describe
- Apply: compose
- Analyze: infer, examine, distinguish, deduce
- Evaluate: decide, evaluate, select, debate, justify
- Create: hypothesize, imagine, suggest, compose

Common Core Standards

College and Career Readiness Anchor Standards, grades 6-9

Reading: RI, R3

Writing: WI, W2, W4, WIO

Speaking & Listening: SLI, SL2, SL3, SL4

Language: LI, L2, L3, L4, L6

What: **Plot Analysis**. Students will show their understanding of how cause and effect impacts the outcome of any situation.

When: Assign after the reading of the story is completed.

Why: Students explore causes and effects in texts. Students use many reading strategies, such as decoding texts, summarizing situations, and clarifying, reflecting, and applying knowledge.

How:

- Use this as an in-class or a homework assignment after students complete the reading.

- Read the instructions aloud and have the students follow along, to make sure that each student understands the tasks that must be completed.

- Students conclude this assignment by comparing and contrasting the author's outcome with their optimal resolution choice. In order to complete this writing segment, students will need to apply the same thinking and reasoning skills that they utilized to complete the chart. This gives teachers the opportunity to assess the students' ability to exhibit their higher-level thinking skills in writing.

TRY THIS *Teachers can use this for a follow-up class discussion for closure, with students reading and explaining their answers.*

IT IS THE CAUSE
"It is the cause, it is the cause, my soul..." (*Othello* V.ii).

Name:_____ Period:_____ Date:_____

Part I: When Othello said this to Desdemona right before he killed her (*Othello,* by William Shakespeare), he couldn't bring himself to state the actual cause of his despair or the reason behind his decision to strangle his beloved wife. For this activity, you have to be stronger than Othello. First, choose three plot situations (one each from the beginning, the middle, and the end) of the story that you are reading. Next, explain the following in the space provided:

1. Describe the cause of the situation/conflict.
2. Identify the reason(s) behind its occurrence.
3. Detail the given effect.
4. Discuss your desired outcome.
5. Analyze the changes necessary for the optional outcome to occur.

	Cause	Reason(s)	Effect	Desired Outcome	Necessary Changes for optional outcome
SITUATION (beginning)					
SITUATION (middle)					
SITUATION (end)					

Part 2: When you are finished with the chart, compare and contrast the author's resolution with your optional outcome. End by explaining which resolution fits the book the best. Justify your points with textual citations.

_____

_____

_____

_____

TEACHER NOTES
Gender Issues

Bloom's Taxonomy

- Remember/Understand: name, explain, identify, describe
- Apply: compose
- Analyze: infer, differentiate, determine, deduce
- Evaluate: conclude, evaluate, debate, justify
- Create: hypothesize, imagine, suppose, compose

Common Core Standards

College and Career Readiness Anchor Standards, grades 6-9

Reading: R1, R3

Writing: W1, W2, W4, W10

Speaking & Listening: SL1, SL2, SL3, SL4

Language: L1, L2, L3, L4, L6

What: **Plot Analysis**. Students explore how gender affects the plot/conflict.

When: This is an excellent warm-up topic after the students have finished the reading. A lively discussion is sure to follow as they share their written responses.

Why: This activity deepens students' comprehension skills, because it requires them to apply critical and analytic thinking skills as they consider a major structural change to the story. They will be led to conclude whether the main conflict would be able to support the story if such a major modification were made.

How:

- Assign this activity as a warm-up topic.
- Allot 15 minutes for the students to complete the writing.
- Lead a whole-class discussion with students summarizing their answers and reading their final paragraph.
- Lead students to discuss the importance of character, plot, and conflict, and why authors make the choices that they do.
- End the class period by asking students to complete an Exit Pass about what they think are the three most important aspects of plot/conflict.

GENDER ISSUES

Name:_____ Period:_____ Date:_____

Change the gender of the main character. How would the story be transformed? Why? Choose three scenes crucial to the climax and explain how they would differ if the main character was of the opposite gender. Consider emotional responses, as well as actions and reactions. End by detailing how the climax would be altered.

Main Conflict: _____
_____
_____
_____

Scene 1: _____
_____
_____
_____

Scene 2: _____
_____
_____
_____

Scene 3: _____
_____
_____
_____

Climax: _____
_____
_____
_____

Final Paragraph: Discuss whether the main conflict would even exist if the characters' genders differed. Explain your answer. _____
_____
_____
_____
_____
_____

TEACHER NOTES
Conflict Connections

Bloom's Taxonomy

- Remember/Understand: name, explain, identify, describe
- Apply: compose
- Analyze: differentiate, examine, determine, categorize
- Evaluate: support, decide, give your opinion, defend,
- Create: compose

Common Core Standards

College and Career Readiness Anchor Standards, grades 6-9

Reading: RI, R3

Writing: WI, W2, W4, WIO

Speaking & Listening: SLI, SL2, SL3, SL4

Language: LI, L2, L3, L4, L6

What: Plot Analysis. Students synthesize their personal experiences and emotions with situations presented in the text.

When: Assign as a concluding activity. Since students finish tests at different times, offer this activity to students as they turn in their assessments. Those who take most of the period for the test can complete it for homework. Either way, hold a follow-up discussion the next class day to conclude this literature study and to lead into the next one.

Why: Requires students to synthesize all of the knowledge they have gained in the study of this literature and incorporate their own life experiences. To accomplish this, they will be remembering/understanding what they read while they apply, analyze, and evaluate their knowledge of plot/conflict.

How:

- Hand out the activity as students turn in their completed tests.
- Students work on them for the remainder of the class and finish them for homework.
- The next class day, each student presents one of his/her responses.

TRY THIS *Segue into the next literature study by choosing a similar conflict in the students' responses and also in the next piece of literature to lead into their introduction for that study. For example, you could say, "A number of you chose the Character vs. Self conflict for Harry Potter in his escapades, Gabby Douglas during her Olympic feats and Katniss Everdeen's adventures in* The Hunger Games. *In the next novel that we will be reading,* The Outsiders, *you'll figure out if Ponyboy Curtis experienced the same conflict." Your examples will reflect your students' choices.*

CONFLICT CONNECTIONS

Name:_____ Period:_____ Date:_____

Choose one of the conflicts from the story that has moved you emotionally. Discuss similar situations in the following areas where you experienced the same feelings. Be sure to address why you felt the way that you did. Give the titles and writers for each category, except for the one detailing a similar situation from your life.

Conflict: _____
_____
_____
_____
_____
_____

Movie: _____
_____
_____
_____
_____
_____

Another Book/Story: _____
_____
_____
_____
_____
_____

News: _____
_____
_____
_____
_____

Song:_____
_____
_____
_____

My Life: _____
_____
_____
_____
_____
_____

TEACHER NOTES
What Kind of World Does the Author Create?

Bloom's Taxonomy

- Remember/Understand: name, explain, identify, describe

- Apply: compose

- Analyze: infer, differentiate, examine, determine

- Evaluate: support, evaluate, select, give your opinion

- Create: hypothesize, suggest, suppose, compose

Common Core Standards

College and Career Readiness Anchor Standards, grades 6-9

Reading: RI, R3

Writing: WI, W2, W4, WIO

Speaking & Listening: SLI, SL2, SL3, SL4

Language: LI, L2, L3, L4, L6

What: **Setting Analysis.** Students will analyze the historical and geographic aspects of the literature, as well as explore societal values, beliefs, and customs.

When: Introduce as soon as the students begin the literature study, and continue from the exposition through the resolution.

Why: Any piece of literature shows not just the geography of the setting, but also illustrates the historical and societal aspects, values, beliefs, and customs of that particular period. Students need to understand that the setting establishes the foundation of the text since the characters, plot, and conflict stem from it. Characters act and react to the situations that arise and, through their development, show the value and belief systems of that time. Students will understand the interplay between the characters, plot, conflict, and setting after they complete this activity.

How:

- Hand out the activity as students begin their reading.

- Allot 5 minutes for students to respond to Part 1, beginning adjective and supporting evidence only.

- Have students discuss the adjectives that they chose and their reasoning. Lead the discussion about how these choices create a mood. This is a good

MORE ⇨

way to get students thinking about the importance of tone in preparation for an in-depth study of this element.

- Allot 10 minutes to complete Part 2.

- Lead a discussion describing the physical and emotional, as well as the societal demands (values, beliefs, customs) of their world. Explain that they will analyze their reading in the same manner.

- Allow students a few minutes the day after each reading segment to add information to Parts 1 and 2, or assign it for homework, requiring students to have it ready for the next day's discussion.

- During the discussions, students can present and defend the examples that they chose.

TRY THIS *Tape up a large piece of newsprint. Every day when the author's world is discussed, students add examples to this sheet (with their initials, so teachers can keep track of who is participating, if desired). After they finish the story, students can organize them in order of importance to the protagonist's life and his/her decisions, actions, and reactions.*

TRY THIS *The writing topic in Part 3 may be completed as closure for the book rather than being turned in for a grade, or it may be used as a formal essay assignment.*

WHAT KIND OF WORLD DOES THE AUTHOR CREATE?

Name:_____ Period:_____ Date:_____

Part 1

Choose an adjective that describes the world the author presents for the beginning, the middle and the end of the book, and then give evidence for each one.

Beginning Adjective_____

Evidence (Include page numbers):

1. _____

_____

_____

2. _____

_____

_____

3. _____

_____

_____

Middle Adjective_____

Evidence (Include page numbers):

1. _____

_____

_____

2. _____

_____

_____

3. _____

_____

_____

End Adjective_____

Evidence (Include page numbers):

1. _____

_____

_____

2. _____

_____

_____

3. _____

_____

_____

Name: _____

Part 2

Detail the type of world the author presents by giving examples for each of the following questions.
After that, explain the acceptance level of the main character (protagonist).

A. What is held sacred in the society?

1. _____

2. _____

Protagonist's level of acceptance: _____

_____

_____

B. What is scorned?

1. _____

2. _____

Protagonist's level of acceptance: _____

_____

_____

C. What are the main customs/traditions?

1. _____

2. _____

3. _____

Protagonist's level of acceptance: _____

_____

_____

D. What are the major beliefs?

1. _____

2. _____

3. _____

Protagonist's level of acceptance: _____

_____

_____

E. What are the expected behaviors?

1. _____

2. _____

3. _____

Protagonist's level of acceptance: _____

_____

_____

Name: _____

Part 3

Develop the following topic in proper paragraph format. Be sure to include a hook to grab the readers, a thesis statement, a minimum of three supporting details and a concluding thought.

How well does the protagonist fit into his/her world? Explain whether or not this person is content with his/her place in the society the author presents.

_____
_____
_____
_____
_____
_____
_____
_____
_____
_____
_____
_____
_____
_____
_____
_____
_____
_____
_____
_____
_____
_____
_____
_____
_____
_____
_____
_____
_____

TEACHER NOTES
Setting It Up

Bloom's Taxonomy

- Remember/Understand: name, explain, identify, describe
- Apply: compose
- Analyze: infer, differentiate, determine, deduce
- Evaluate: conclude, support, evaluate, give your opinion, justify
- Create: hypothesize, imagine, compose

Common Core Standards

College and Career Readiness Anchor Standards, grades 6-9

Reading: R1, R3

Writing: W1, W2, W4, W10

Speaking & Listening: SL1, SL2, SL3, SL4

Language: L1, L2, L3, L4, L6

What: **Setting Analysis**. Following the ten-sentence format on this activity, students will show their understanding of their reading and of setting to compose a paragraph.

When: After students complete the reading.

Why: Requires students to synthesize all of the knowledge they have gained in the study of this literature with their own life experiences.

How:

- Assign this as the warm-up topic the day after the reading is completed.
- Review the parts of a paragraph with the students, if necessary.
- Allot students 15 to 20 minutes to complete the writing.
- Have two or three students read their paragraphs aloud.
- Discuss how the protagonist or antagonist had to change to fit the new setting.
- Lead students to make conclusions about the importance of setting.

SETTING IT UP

Name:_____ Period:_____ Date:_____

Complete this activity using the Ten Sentence Format. The numbers in parentheses show the point value for each segment.

Situation: Put the protagonist or the antagonist (your choice) from this reading in a setting that is totally different from the one depicted in the story. You select the time period. Show how the dissimilar setting would change the character's beliefs, actions, and reactions to a situation that is similar to one he/she faced in the book.

Hook: _____

_____ (1)

Overview Statement: _____

_____ (1)

Thesis statement: _____

_____ (3)

Main Idea 1: _____

_____ (3)

Supporting Detail #1 w/example: _____

_____ (2)

Main Idea 2: _____

_____ (3)

Supporting Detail #2 w/example: _____

_____ (2)

Main Idea 3: _____

_____ (3)

Supporting Detail #3 w/ example: _____

_____ (2)

Concluding Statement: _____

_____

_____ (5)

TEACHER NOTES
Green Light! Red Light!

Bloom's Taxonomy

- Remember/Understand: observe, explain, give examples
- Apply: choose, show
- Analyze: distinguish, infer, examine
- Evaluate: give your opinion, defend, summarize
- Create: describe, state, suggest, hypothesize

Common Core Standards

College and Career Readiness Anchor Standards, grades 6-9

Reading: R1, R2, R3, R4, R5, R6

Writing: W1, W2, W10

Language: L1, L2

What: **Reading Comprehension**

When: As they proceed through the reading.

Why: Teachers should periodically check the students' comprehension of the reading in order to tweak their lesson plans to include student-specific reading strategies or to reinforce students' understanding of any of the elements of literature. This is also a good way for teachers to see which students are up-to-date with their reading.

How:

- For reading done in class, students should complete one five-minute round of reading at the beginning of the period, followed by a five-minute writing session and a five-minute "End of the Road" writing. Follow it with a question/answer session to explain and clarify any confusion.

- If students are expected to complete the reading for homework, have them read in class for five minutes at the end of the period and then complete a five-minute writing session. They can continue their reading at home as assigned and complete an "End of the Road" writing during the warm-up session at the beginning of the next class or for homework.

- If teacher wants to spend the majority of a class period checking the students' comprehension, have the students complete three five-minute rounds of reading, each followed by a five-minute writing session. Then finish with the "End of the Road" segment (five minutes), for a total of 35 minutes.

MORE ⇨

- Teacher calls out, "Green light!" to signal the start of the five-minute reading period, and "Red light!" to signal the end of the five minutes of reading. Then teacher starts to time the next five minutes while students write, answering the activity questions, calling "Green light!" and "Red light!" to signal the start and end of writing. Then two more rounds of "Green Light! Red Light!" are played. Finally, the teacher says, "End of the road!" which signals the students to spend five minutes writing three conclusions based on the reading.

- After checking the students' results of the "Green light! Red Light!" activity, teacher assesses the students' comprehension levels and chooses additional activities for those who need more practice.

TRY THIS *This activity can also be used as a ten-minute warm-up each of three days following a homework reading assignment. Students would complete one round of reading and writing and the "End of the Road" segment each time.*

GRADING SUGGSTION *Teachers could grade the students on their completion of this activity. Example: three points for addressing each of the three issues; two points for addressing two issues and one point for addressing only one issue. Two points should be given for the "End of the Road" section. The grade should only be for completing the required writing.*

GREEN LIGHT! RED LIGHT!

Name:_____ Period:_____ Date:_____

When the teacher says, "Green light!" start reading. When the teacher says, "Red light!" stop reading and write in the space below. Each time you write, comment on the following:

- Who is doing what to/with whom? Why?
- What emotions are the characters revealing?
- Where is this scene taking place?

Round 1: Reading (5 minutes)

Book: _____ Pages Read: _____

Round 1: Writing (5 minutes)

_____
_____
_____
_____

Round 2: Reading (5 minutes)

Book: _____ Pages Read: _____

Round 1: Writing (5 minutes)

_____
_____
_____
_____

Round 3: Reading (5 minutes)

Book: _____ Pages Read: _____

Round 3: Writing (5 minutes)

_____
_____
_____
_____

End of the Road: Write three conclusions that you have reached about the characters and conflict after today's reading.

1. _____

2. _____

3. _____

TEACHER NOTES
Journal Response Letters

Bloom's Taxonomy

- **Remember/Understand:** Many of the verbs work here because written conversations are wide open for student discussion choices.

- **Apply:** describe, discuss, explain, understand

- **Analyze:** infer, compare, contrast, distinguish, determine

- **Evaluate:** discuss, conclude, support, judge, justify

- **Create:** imagine, hypothesize, suggest, debate

Common Core Standards

College and Career Readiness Anchor Standards, grades 6-9

Reading: R1, R2, R3, R4, R5, R6

Writing: W1, W2, W10

Language: L1, L2, L3

What: **Reading Comprehension.** Students are paired with another student reading the same text, and they correspond anonymously about what they are reading. Their "conversations" are only in writing. Students who are paired together can be on different ability/skill levels. The students' written conversations should deal with several textual and literary issues.

When: While students are reading a novel or novella. It is best used when multiple classes are reading the same book, because the teacher can pair a student from one class with a student in another class. This helps keep their writing anonymous, allowing them to be more open and honest with concerns or questions than they might be during oral discussions. It can also be used effectively within one class, but teachers need to make sure that each student has the same type/color of composition book in order to keep identities secret.

Why: This activity provides students with a chance to discuss the book risk-free. They can speak openly about what they are reading, ask questions about scenes that they don't understand, and present their thoughts and opinions without any reservations. Teachers can assess students' textual and elements of literature understanding daily.

MORE ➡

How:

- Randomly assign numbers to students; keep a master list of the numbers.
- Important: students should not learn the identity of their journal partner.
- Do as a daily warm-up following each homework reading assignment.
- Day 1: each student writes an entry.
- From Day 2 to the end of the book, each student responds to the partner's entry and addresses any points, observations, or questions from the partner.

TRY THIS *Use manila folders and fill them with lined paper. Only the student numbers go on the folders; the teachers keep a master list of students and their numbers. Students should write after each reading session.*

GRADING SUGGESTIONS

Teachers can decide:

- Word minimums
- Grading values
- Number of entries to be completed
- How to handle missing work from absent students.

Example:

- A minimum of 150 words is worth 75%; 200 words is worth 84%; 250 words is worth 100%.
- Ten entries should be completed before the day of the test.
- If students are absent and letters are missed, the teacher will decide if any letters can be made up after discussing the missing work with the parents.

JOURNAL RESPONSE LETTERS

You will correspond with another student in this or another class who is reading the same book.

1. After every reading assignment, write a letter to the person with whom you are paired, addressing one or two of the criteria points, as well as anything else you might want to say about the story (keep it positive, even if you express complaints).

2. You will be assigned a number, as will be the person you are writing to, so this exercise stays completely anonymous. Address your letters to this number. Sign your letter with the number assigned to you. NO NAMES and NO DECORATING THE FOLDERS, as that may reveal your identity. The anonymity encourages you to express your thoughts and feelings more freely.

3. Number each letter consecutively. Make sure that your letter is on a separate sheet of paper from your partner's.

4. The teacher will collect the letters at the end of each class to distribute to your partner.

5. You will get your partner's letter back during the next class so you can respond to what he/she wrote.

6. This process will continue until we finish discussing the story. On the day of the test, you will turn in all of the letters for a grade.

7. If you don't receive a letter from your partner, write about one of the criteria points.

Criteria:

- What intrigued you in this section?

- What don't you understand that you want explained? Ask your partner for help.

- What do you predict will happen in the next section?

- Describe how you felt after reading the assigned pages.

- Speak to any points your partner raises.

- Keep your content appropriate and grammatically correct.

- Keep to the topic; do not spend this time socializing with your partner.

- Number and date each entry, and write a title that shows your focus.

TEACHER NOTES
What Was I Thinking?

Bloom's Taxonomy

- Remember/Understand: describe, discuss, explain, identify
- Apply: compose
- Analyze: infer, differentiate, deduce, examine
- Evaluate: discuss, conclude, support, appraise, justify
- Create: imagine, hypothesize, suggest, compose

Common Core Standards

College and Career Readiness Anchor Standards, grades 6-9

Reading: R1, R2, R4, R5

Writing: W1, W2, W10

Speaking & Listening: SL1, SL2, SL3, SL4

Language: L1, L2, L3, L4

What: **Reading Comprehension.** Students' answers will range from emotional and opinionated to factual and analytical as they address the points in this activity.

When: Use once the characters, plot/conflict, and setting have been firmly established. Although symbols and theme may have been introduced, they might not be clarified at this point in the text. If they have been, students should feel free to address them in their answers. Any point from the latter part of the rising action would be a good place to introduce this handout.

Why: Requires students to address what they have read in a complex manner, helping them to build their higher-level thinking skills as they show a deeper analysis of the elements of literature.

How:

- Students should complete questions 1, 2, 3, and 4 independently. Allot students fifteen minutes to complete 1 through 4.

- Students break into groups of four or less and address question 5. Allot ten minutes for group discussion of question 5.

- Students then work independently to answer question 6. Allot five minutes for students to write their responses to question 6.

- After the students have completed question 6, begin a whole class discussion. Ask for volunteers to summarize their answers for questions 1 through 4.

- Write *Characters, Plot/Conflict, Setting, Tone,* and *Point of View* on the board and have students discuss how they intertwine. Draw lines between the elements to illustrate the meshing. Discuss which elements are given more clarity and complexity because of the influence of other elements.

WHAT WAS I THINKING?

Name:_____ Period:_____ Date:_____

Students: Select up to one paragraph of text that is particularly troubling and/or confusing, yet also intriguing. Copy it in the space below, and then respond independently to questions 1 through 4.

Citation (include page number): _____

_____

_____

_____

_____

1. (Emotional Response): Describe your personal response. What emotions did you experience when reading it? Address any personal experience where you felt the same emotions.

_____

_____

_____

_____

2. (Intellectual Response): What ideas came to mind as you read this? What questions does this passage raise regarding humans? About life or the state of the world? What is the author trying to say? Rephrase the passage as you would say it.

_____

_____

_____

_____

3. Relate the ideas in the passage to other parts of the story. Discuss the connections.

_____

_____

_____

_____

4. (Reacting as a writer): What do you notice about the way the passage is written? What appeals? What doesn't? Why? Consider word choices and sentence structure in your answer.

_____

_____

_____

_____

Break into assigned groups to respond to question 5.

5. Share your answers to questions 1 through 4, as well as why you chose them. Jot down points the group members make that expand your thinking.

_____

_____

_____

_____

Respond independently to question 6.

6. Summarize the group's discussion in one or two sentences. Then, re-analyze your thoughts in questions 1 - 4. Consider the following when you respond: Did you change your mind about your original response? How? Why? What clarifications did you receive? Did you find another person's passage more intriguing? If so, explain. What did you learn about another passage that had previously confused you?

_____

_____

_____

_____

_____

_____

_____

_____

TEACHER NOTES
Author, Author, What's Your Purpose?

Bloom's Taxonomy

- Remember/Understand: describe, discuss, explain, identify,
- Apply: compose, illustrate
- Analyze: infer, differentiate, deduce, examine
- Evaluate: conclude, support, decide, appraise,
- Create: suggest, suppose, compose

Common Core Standards

College and Career Readiness Anchor Standards, grades 6-9

Reading: R1, R2

Writing: W1, W2, W10

Language: L1, L2, L3, L4

What: Reading Comprehension.

When: During the falling action discussion but before they have read the resolution.

Why: Students demonstrate their analytic and interpretive thinking skills that allow them to deconstruct the story for each element. After analyzing the students' responses, teachers can refer to the Unit Structure and Comprehension Activities charts (Chapter 1) to assess which elements need more reinforcement.

How:

- Assign this for homework during the falling action discussion but before they have read the resolution. Allot 2 days to complete this activity.

- Students must turn it in the day the class discusses the resolution so teachers can assess the students' understanding of the correlation between the text and the elements of literature.

TRY THIS *If this activity is used as an assignment for a short story, hand it out when students begin reading, so they can complete it as they read.*

AUTHOR, AUTHOR, WHAT'S YOUR PURPOSE?

Name:_____ Period:_____ Date:_____

Writers have a purpose for everything that they include in a story. For the one that you are reading, find examples of the following writing techniques that authors employ to add depth to a story, and complete the directions for each task in complete sentences.

Title: _____ Author: _____

1. A reference to a significant past event that impacted the protagonist's thoughts/ beliefs/actions:
   Event: _____
   _____
   Impact: _____
   _____

2. A reference to a significant past event that impacted the antagonist's thoughts/ beliefs/actions:
   Event: _____
   _____
   Impact: _____
   _____

3. Lines that foreshadow a future event (copy the exact citation).
   Citation: _____
   _____
   Future Event: _____
   _____

4. A quote by the protagonist that revealed one of his/her personality or physical traits.
   Quote:_____
   _____
   Trait: _____
   _____

5. A quote by the antagonist that revealed one of his/her personality or physical traits.
   Quote:_____
   _____
   Trait: _____
   _____

6. A quote by a secondary character that revealed one of the protagonist's personality or physical traits.
   Quote:_____
   _____
   Trait: _____
   _____

7. A quote by a secondary character that revealed one of the antagonist's personality or physical traits.
   Quote: _____

   _____

   Trait: _____

   _____

8. Three citations that helped create the mood.
   A. Citation: _____

   _____

   Mood: _____

   _____

   B. Citation: _____

   _____

   Mood: _____

   _____

   C. Citation: _____

   _____

   Mood: _____

   _____

9. A quote by a character that shows he/she is attempting to evade an issue.
   Quote: _____

   _____

   Issue: _____

   _____

10. A quote where a character attempts to conceal his/her thoughts or feelings.
    Quote: _____

    _____

    What he/she wants to hide: _____

    _____

11. Explain how the setting impacts the plot/conflict and resolution.

    _____

    _____

    _____

    _____

12. A situation that reveals the primary conflict (Man vs. What?) the protagonist faces.
    Situation: _____

    _____

    Conflict: _____

13. Identify a major symbol and explain what it represents.

Symbol: _____

_____

What it represents: _____

_____

14. Summarize the climactic event—the point of no return for the protagonist. Explain the protagonist's decision and show how the plot/conflict is affected.

Climactic event: _____

_____

Decision: _____

_____

15. Identify the theme, which is the universal message the author imparts in the story. Explain your answer.

Theme: _____

_____

Explanation: _____

_____

CHAPTER 4

THE FINISH WORK

The finish carpentry in the building process is what gives a house its personality. The trim is added, cabinets are built, and the details make the house come alive.

Like the finish work in a house, literature includes elements that add complexity and dynamism. A story's theme, symbols, point of view, and tone add more layers to comprehension because they comprise the subtext of a literary work. They are not objective (factual) in nature, but are subjective (based on opinion). They require students to intellectually engage in the reading through their interpretations, inferences, and analyses. Higher-level thinking skills are necessary when students read and decode more complicated textual material.

Exercises that require students to make connections between the text and their own lives deepen their comprehension of the material. Studying the elements of theme, symbols, point of view, and tone offers learners the opportunity to question, analyze, reflect, and apply their knowledge. The activities in this chapter will help students strengthen the analytic skills necessary to interpret the subtexts in literature.

MODULES

Analyzing Theme
- What's in a Theme?
- If the Theme Fits... Use It!

Analyzing Symbols
- Symbols Hold the Key
- Symbols: They Represent

Analyzing Point of View and Tone
- What's Your Point?
- Starring... ME!
- Let's Tone Up

TEACHER NOTES
What's In a Theme?

Bloom's Taxonomy

• Remember/Understand: name, explain, identify, describe

• Analyze: differentiate, examine, determine, categorize

• Evaluate: conclude, support, evaluate, select,

• Create: suggest, suppose, compose

Common Core Standards

College and Career Readiness Anchor Standards, grades 6-9

Reading: RI, R2, R9, RIO

Writing: WI, W2, WIO

Speaking & Listening: SLI, SL2, SL3, SL4

Language: LI, L2, L3, L6

What: **Theme Analysis**. Students learn the difference between a theme and a theme topic. They will analyze and evaluate previously read works of literature and create theme statements.

When: Present this activity during the falling action or resolution segments of the piece. By this time, the author's universal message (theme) should be clear.

Why: In every piece of literature, whether it is fiction, non-fiction, or poetry, authors have a universal message they present and develop throughout the piece. Students need to be able to differentiate between the theme topic (communication, war, alienation, etc.) and the theme (the statement the author is making about the topic, i.e., "In war, everyone loses"), which is a subjective premise. They will learn that the theme is the glue that holds all of the elements of literature together.

How:

- Allot 15 minutes for students to complete **What's In a Theme?**

- Have several students present their theme topic, example, and theme.

- Have students write the theme on the board that they hypothesized for the current literature under study.

- From these examples, students can select one or two themes for the text they are currently reading while the teacher guides their reasoning by having them support their choices with textual evidence.

WHAT'S IN A THEME?

Name:_____ Period:_____ Date:_____

    A theme by any other name...well, it sure wouldn't be a theme.

    A theme is a statement that the author makes about people and their interactions with others and the world. Although an author's characters, plot/conflict, and setting are developed and inter-woven throughout the text, these elements are glued together by the theme—the author's purpose for writing. One major message will prevail. This is the theme of the book. It must be written as a complete statement, not as a phrase. A theme topic presents a general idea; it does *not* make a state-ment about that issue.

Directions:

Part 1: For each of the 10 theme topics, write the name of a book/short story that you have read inde-pendently (not a required book), and give an example from the piece that supports that theme topic.

Part 2: Choose one theme topic and example from Part 1 and then write the theme.

Next, suggest a theme for the story that we are currently studying in class, and write it where indicated.

Part 1

Theme Topics	Book/Story	Supporting Example
1. Choices in life		
2. Coming of age		
3. Conflict of cultures		
4. The individual and society		
5. Life and loss		
6. Nature of evil		
7. The power of pain and love		
8. Triumph and defeat		
9. Uses and abuses of power		
10. Loss and innocence		

Part 2

Examples of themes:

- The lack of communication can lead to tragedy (*Romeo and Juliet*).
- In war, everyone loses (*The Things They Carried*; *All Quiet on the Western Front*).
- If he chooses, man can overcome any hurdle or hardship (*The Odyssey*).

Theme from Part 1:

_____

_____

_____

Theme of current story:

_____

_____

_____

TEACHER NOTES
If the Theme Fits...Use It!

Bloom's Taxonomy

- Remember/Understand: name, explain, identify, describe
- Analyze: examine, distinguish, determine, deduce
- Evaluate: support, select, give your opinion, defend
- Create: suggest, compose

Common Core Standards

College and Career Readiness Anchor Standards, grades 6-9

Reading: RI, R2, R7, R9, RIO

Writing: WI, W2, W8, WIO

Speaking & Listening: SLI, SL2, SL3, SL4

Language: LI, L2, L3, L6

What: **Theme Analysis.** Students will have to fully dissect the theme of the text and be able to evaluate other books, movies, songs, and television shows that send the same message.

When: Present this activity during the falling action or resolution segments of the piece they are studying, but after they complete the **What's in a Theme?** activity and discussion.

Why: This activity requires learners to exhibit a comprehensive understanding of theme. By the time they have completed this exercise, they should see how the theme ties together the characters, plot/conflict, and setting that the author develops in the literature.

How:

- Break the class into groups of three.
- Hand out copies of the activity—one per student, and one for each group to present to the class as a final copy.
- Allot 20 minutes for the completion of this activity.
- Have students initial the choices, evidence, and explanations that they contributed.
- When the time is up, have each member of the group orally present one of the choices as well as the evidence and explanation.

MORE ⇨

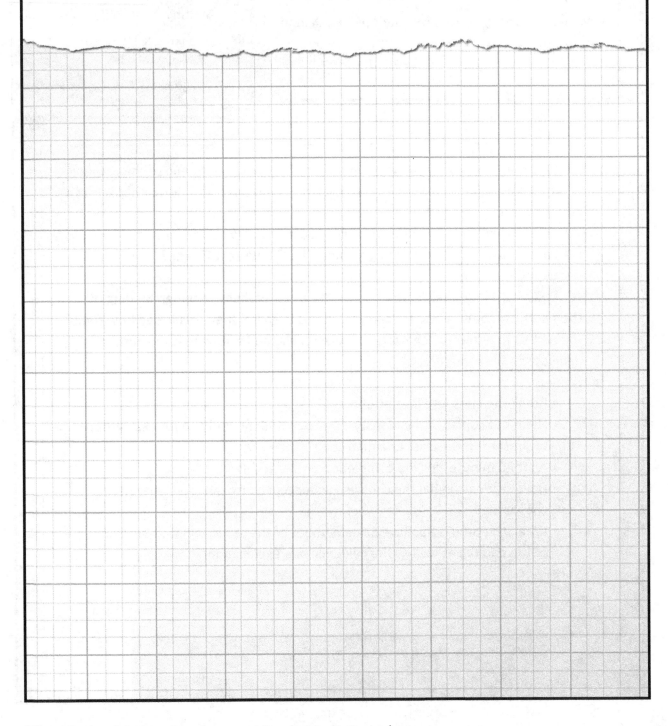

TRY THIS *After the teacher visually checks the activity for completion, he/she can post the finished group sheets (not the students' individual sheets) on the bulletin board so students can read and discuss their peers' choices. Students love to discuss movies, books, etc., and this way they can practice verbalizing their choices and their supporting evidence. Also, since every group addresses a different theme, the conversations can offer clarity to students who might still be confused about writing and supporting theme statements.*

IF THE THEME FITS... USE IT!

Name:_____ Period:_____ Date:_____

In groups of three, write the theme of the text you are studying in the space below. Choose other books, movies, songs, or television shows with the same theme. Be sure to include specific evidence and explanations that clarify the connection to the theme.

Theme:_____
_____

Choice	Evidence	Explanation
1.		
2.		
3.		
4.		
5.		
6.		
7.		
8.		
9.		
10.		
11.		
12.		
13.		
14.		

TEACHER NOTES
Symbols Hold the Key

Bloom's Taxonomy

- Remember/Understand: name, explain, identify, describe

- Apply: draw, compose

- Analyze: infer, examine, determine, deduce

- Evaluate: conclude, support, evaluate, give your opinion, defend

- Create: hypothesize, suggest, compose

Common Core Standards

College and Career Readiness Anchor Standards, grades 6-9

Reading: RI, R2, R4, R7, RIO

Writing: WI, W2, W9, WIO

Speaking & Listening: SLI, SL2, SL3, SL4

Language: LI, L2, L3, L6

What: **Symbol Analysis.** Students analyze symbols from literature and life, explaining their meanings and where and why each exists. They will apply their knowledge and understanding of symbols to the text they are currently reading.

When: This study can begin during the rising action of the text and continue through the end of the reading, with students adding to their symbols list in Part 4 as they read and discuss the piece.

Why: Symbols add a more complex layer to comprehension. They require students to intellectually engage in the reading through their interpretations, inferences, and analyses. Any reading requires students to make connections between the text and their own lives to deepen their understanding. Studying symbols allows them to question, analyze, reflect, and apply this knowledge and understanding. Since a character, conflict, setting, or plot aspect may be a symbol, this activity shows students how the elements of literature never stand alone as separate entities.

How:

- Distribute the activity. Read the first paragraph aloud to explain symbols and review the six symbols for examples.

- For more discussion, ask students to name and explain symbols from other texts they have studied.

- Allot 5 minutes for students to complete Part 1. Discuss their answers.

- Next, allot 5 minutes for Part 2. Discuss.

MORE ➡

- For Part 3, have students begin to list and explain symbols from their current reading. Students will add to this chart as they continue their study of the literature.

- Require students to turn in this activity on a specified day; usually, the review day is appropriate.

GRADING SUGGESTIONS *Assign a value for each point students must address in Part 3. For example: 2 points for naming the symbol; 3 for telling where and why it exists, and 5 for explaining the meaning. Extra credit is the teacher's choice.*

SYMBOLS HOLD THE KEY

Name:_____ Period:_____ Date:_____

Symbols occur in most creative works: short stories, novels, poetry, music (lyrics and instrumentals), personal narratives, and art, to name just a few genres. They enhance a piece by taking it to a deeper level. Not every person, place, thing, or idea in a work (i.e., an object, a season, the weather, a color), is a symbol. Sometimes they are just part of the narrative development. To be symbols, they should clearly stand for a specific person, place, thing, or idea and connect to the theme.

Here are some symbols from novels:

Novel	Object	Symbolizes
Animal Farm	Ribbons	Vanity
Night	Violin	Beauty and defiance
Othello	Handkerchief	Fidelity
One Flew Over the Cuckoo's Nest	Geese	Freedom
The Odyssey	Food	Temptation
The Crucible	Gold Candlesticks	Materialism

Part I:

Draw three well-known symbols and explain what they stand for:

	_____ _____ _____ _____
	_____ _____ _____ _____
	_____ _____ _____ _____

Name: _____

Part 2:
On the spaces below each image, (1) name the symbol, (2) tell where/why it exists and (3) explain its meaning:

(image)	(image)	(image)
1._____ 2._____ _____ 3._____ _____	1._____ 2._____ _____ 3._____ _____	1._____ 2._____ _____ 3._____ _____

Part 3:
Search your reading for symbols. For each one that you find, complete the following:

Name the symbol: _____ _____ Tell where/why it exists: _____ _____ Explain its meaning: _____ _____ **Extra Credit**: Draw a picture of the symbol: ➯	
Name the symbol: _____ _____ Tell where/why it exists: _____ _____ Explain its meaning: _____ _____ **Extra Credit**: Draw a picture of the symbol: ➯	
Name the symbol: _____ _____ Tell where/why it exists: _____ _____ Explain its meaning: _____ _____ **Extra Credit**: Draw a picture of the symbol: ➯	

TEACHER NOTES
Symbols: They Represent!

Bloom's Taxonomy

- Remember/Understand: name, explain, identify; describe

- Apply: illustrate, draw, compose

- Analyze: infer, distinguish, determine, deduce

- Evaluate: conclude, support, evaluate, give your opinion, defend

- Create: hypothesize, suggest, compose

Common Core Standards

College and Career Readiness Anchor Standards, grades 6-9

Reading: RI, R2, R4, R8, RIO

Writing: WI, W2, W9, WIO

Speaking & Listening: SLI, SL2, SL3, SL4

Language: LI, L2, L3, L6

What: Symbol Analysis. Students will analyze one of the symbols from Part 3 of the **Symbols Hold the Key** activity.

When: Complete during the falling action segment of the reading. All the symbols should be clearly developed at this point.

Why: Students will further develop their understanding of symbols while following the **Ten Sentence Format** (see p. 41), which lends itself to expansion from a paragraph into a full essay.

How:

- Assign this activity as an in-class exercise during the falling action.

- Allot 20 to 30 minutes for students to complete the writing, depending on their comprehension and writing skills.

GRADING SUGGESTION *Teachers can use this activity to assess not only the students' comprehension of symbols, but also to analyze their understanding of the parts of a paragraph.*

After they assess the students' writing, teachers can:

1. Reinforce the elements of a paragraph through individual or group critiques, and/or

2. Have students turn the paragraph into a full-length essay.

SYMBOLS: THEY REPRESENT!

Name:_____ Period:_____ Date:_____

Directions:

Draw or find a picture that fits one of the symbols in the book. Write an explanation explaining what the symbol represents using the ten-sentence format. The point values for each segment are in parentheses; 25 points total. ➪

Hook: _____
_____ (1)

Overview Statement:_____
_____ (1)

Thesis Statement: _____
_____
_____ (3)

Main Idea 1:_____
_____
_____ (3)

Supporting Detail #1 with example: _____
_____
_____
_____ (2)

Main Idea 2:_____
_____
_____ (3)

Supporting Detail #2 with example: _____
_____
_____
_____ (2)

Main Idea 3:_____
_____
_____ (3)

Supporting Detail #3 with example: _____
_____
_____
_____ (2)

Concluding Statement: _____
_____
_____ (5)

TEACHER NOTES
What's Your Point?

Bloom's Taxonomy

- Remember/Understand: name, explain, identify, describe
- Apply: compose
- Analyze: examine, distinguish, determine, categorize
- Evaluate: support, select, give your opinion, defend
- Create: hypothesize, imagine, suppose, compose

Common Core Standards

College and Career Readiness Anchor Standards, grades 6-9

Reading: RI, R2, R6

Writing: WI, W2, W3, W4, W5, WI0

Speaking & Listening: SLI, SL2, SL3, SL4

Language: LI, L2, L3, L6

What: Point of View Analysis

When: After the initial reading segment.

Why: Students need to learn that the point of view the author chooses for a story is one of the most important and influential elements of literature. What readers understand about the characters, plot, conflict, setting, theme, and symbols is dependent on who is telling the story. Judgments that readers make about the elements of literature are influenced by what the narrator wants them to see. Word choices and sentence structures are made accordingly.

How:

- Before starting this lesson, prepare a number of specific situations on separate slips of paper that have two people involved. These situations should be ones the students can relate to—perhaps ones that mirror their lives. The number of situations should equal half the number of students in the class. Create one situation with three participants for odd-numbered classes.

  EXAMPLES OF SITUATIONS:

  A. A teenage boy and a 45-year-old female witness a car crash at an intersection by the high school. A 17-year-old female was driving the car and a 65-year-old man was driving the other.

  B. Two girls witness a male underclassman being bullied by the boyfriend of one of the girls.

  C. Two football spectators, each one a fan of one of the two teams, defends/challenges a referee's controversial call.

MORE ⇨

- Pair up students (one trio, if needed). Give each pair one of the slips of paper. Instruct each student to adopt the persona of one of the situation's participants and then explain the event from that person's point of view.
- Allot 5 minutes for students to write their observations of the situations.
- When they are done, have a few students read their observations aloud; lead them to see the differences in interpretations.
- Distribute the **What's Your Point?** activity sheets.
- Discuss the types of narrators by reviewing the chart.
- Part 1: review the directions together and then divide students into groups of five. Allot 5 minutes for the writing part of this exercise and 15-20 minutes for the presentation segment (3-4 minutes per group for five groups).
- Part 2 should be assigned for homework.
- Part 3 can be completed when teachers want to reinforce the importance of point of view.

TRY THIS *Orally and in writing, students can critique one another's paragraphs from Parts 2 and 3. Doing so will address Common Core Speaking, Listening, and Language Standards.*

TRY THIS *Use the ten-sentence format for Parts 2 and 3 to reinforce how to write a paragraph.*

WHAT'S YOUR POINT?

To *narrate* means to relate the details about an event or situation. The person who does this is the Narrator. Sometimes, the Narrator is a participant in the story. Other times, the Narrator tells about what happened, but is not a part of the situation. More often than not, the Narrator is omniscient, meaning he/she knows all the details about who is doing what to whom as well as when, how, and why for every character. Sometimes the Narrator is limited, meaning he/she knows everything about only the main character. Neither type of Narrator is a part of the action, though.

Types of Narrators

First Person	• Uses first person singular: *I, me, my.* • Occasionally uses first person plural: *we, our.* • Is almost always the main character in the story; very rarely, this person tells the story but is not its focus.
Third Limited	• Always relates the story in third person singular or plural: *he, she, it, they.* • This Narrator is *not* a character in the story; he/she knows everything about only one character (usually the main character)
Third Omniscient	• Always relates the story in third person singular or plural: *he, she, it, they.* • This Narrator is a know-it-all. No dirty little secrets with this non-participant.
Second Person	• A rarely-seen entity, this Narrator talks to the reader, "You must remember what happened as well as I do." • Although readers may encounter this type of storyteller, you should NEVER write in this point of view. The second person point of view should only be used for giving directions or instructing the reader about a process.

WHAT'S YOUR POINT?
Part 1

Name: _____ Period: _____ Date: _____

In groups of five, complete the chart.

1. Choose the leader.

2. Starting with the leader, and then moving clockwise, each group member fills in the information for Title, Author, Main Character, and Narrator for a book or short story he/she read in school or on his/her own in the past year.

3. The leader will present this information to the rest of the class. Each group member will participate by explaining the type of narrator the author used in the story.

Title	Author	Main Character	Narrator

Part 2:

In ten sentences, tell the story of *Little Red Riding Hood* from the point of view of the wolf, or *Twilight* from the point of view of Edward.

_____

_____

_____

_____

_____

_____

_____

_____

_____

_____

_____

_____

_____

_____

_____

_____

_____

_____

_____

_____

_____

_____

_____

_____

_____

_____

_____

_____

_____

Part 3:

Take the story that we are currently reading in class. Choose your favorite scene so far, and show one page of it from the point of view of a different type of narrator. For example, if the story is being told in third person limited, write it from third omniscient or first person. Then write a paragraph explaining which point of view works better and why.

_____

_____

_____

_____

_____

_____

_____

_____

_____

_____

_____

_____

_____

_____

_____

_____

_____

_____

_____

_____

_____

_____

_____

_____

_____

_____

_____

_____

TEACHER NOTES
Starring... ME!

Bloom's Taxonomy

- Remember/Understand: name, explain, identify, describe
- Apply: compose
- Analyze: differentiate, examine, determine, deduce
- Evaluate: decide, evaluate, select, give your opinion
- Create: hypothesize, compose

Common Core Standards

College and Career Readiness Anchor Standards, grades 6-9

Reading: RI, R2, R6, R10

Writings: W1, W2, W3, W4, W5, W9, W10

Speaking & Listening: SL1, SL2, SL3, SL4

Language: L1, L2, L3, L6

What: Point of View Analysis. Students will become the protagonist in the story but keep his/her own point of view (POV).

When: Teachers should assign this during the latter part of the rising action, but before the climax of the story.

Why: In order to fully comprehend the importance of POV, students need to see how a piece of literature would transform if the narrator held a different POV. This assignment requires students to process information, to question the narrator's POV, and to utilize higher-level thinking and reasoning skills to create a different version.

How:

- Hand out this assignment during the latter part of the rising action, but before the climax of the story. This activity can be done as an in-class assignment or as homework, whichever fits best into the teachers' unit agendas.

- When they have finished the writing, teachers should group the students by threes. Students will take turns reading their writing to the others and will discuss how the resolution would change. They should also discuss whether or not they agree with the changes, which will result in deeper comprehension.

TRY THIS *Reinforce the importance of the narrator by asking students to role-play. Throughout the reading, ask students to take on the persona of the narrator. They can do this orally by explaining what information is limited to that type of narrator. For a writing and speaking exercise, if the story is written in first person, ask students to write a teacher-selected paragraph from the POV of a third omniscient narrator. Select two or three students to read their paragraphs.*

STARRING... ME!

Name:_____ Period:_____ Date:_____

You have been chosen to be the main character in the story that you are reading in class. Instead of adopting that character's personality, beliefs and values, you are able to keep *your* point of view and to apply it to the actions and reactions in the situations that the character (now *you*) encountered. How would the story change with this different point of view? Choose five situations that are crucial to the outcome of the story, summarize them, and explain what you would have said or done. Show how all of these choices would affect the outcome of the story. What would be the final outcome?

Character:

_____

Story:

_____

Author:

_____

```
+------------------+
|                  |
|       Your       |
|      Picture     |
|       here       |
|                  |
+------------------+
```

Situation 1:_____

_____

Your actions, reactions, thoughts:_____

_____

Situation 2:_____

_____

Your actions, reactions, thoughts:_____

_____

Situation 3:_____

_____

Your actions, reactions, thoughts:_____

_____

Situation 4:_____

_____

Your actions, reactions, thoughts:_____

_____

Situation 5:_____

_____

Your actions, reactions, thoughts:_____

_____

Final Outcome:_____

_____

TEACHER NOTES
Pairing Up

Bloom's Taxonomy

- **Remember/Understand:** name, explain, identify, describe
- **Apply:** compose, dramatize
- **Analyze:** infer, examine, distinguish, determine
- **Evaluate:** support, evaluate, select, give your opinion
- **Create:** hypothesize, imagine, suppose, compose

Common Core Standards

College and Career Readiness Anchor Standards, grades 6-9

Reading: R1, R3, R6

Writing: W1, W2, W4, W10

Speaking & Listening: SL1, SL2, SL3, SL4

Language: L1, L2, L3, L4, L6

What: Point of View Development. Students will adopt a character's point of view to write a dialogue.

When: This activity should be assigned at any point in the story prior to the resolution.

Why: This activity requires students to understand the relationship between the elements of literature in order to write detailed dialogues. After completing this assignment, teachers can assess how well their students understand the relationship between the elements of literature and decide which students need specific elements reinforced.

How:

- Before the class meets, teacher prepares examples of situations from the story for each of the following: inciting moment, rising action, climax, falling action, and resolution. Although there will be only one each of the inciting moment, climax, and resolution, prepare as many situations in the rising action and falling action so the total number of plot examples is equal to half the number of students. Write each situation on a separate slip of paper.

- Pair up students, with each one assuming the persona of a character from the book. Don't be concerned about students getting a character of the same gender. In fact, it stretches their thinking for them to deduce how a person of the opposing sex would think and act.

- The characters will appear multiple times. Make sure there are no identical pairs. For a class with an uneven number, there will be one trio, or one person can write a monologue. (Example: in a class of 25, there will be 11 pairs and one trio or 12 pairs and one monologue.)

MORE ⇨

- Each pair chooses one slip of paper, and then discusses the situation and the characters' actions and reactions to the event.

- Next, the pair writes a dialogue with each student writing from the point of view of his/her character by passing the activity back and forth after each response.

- In their dialogues, students must reveal their character's personality and interpret his/her feelings, actions and reactions. What students illustrate with their words should reveal their interpretations of the characters, not those of the author of the story.

- Allot 20-25 minutes for students to complete this assignment.

- When completed, the student pairs read their dialogues to the class.

TRY THIS *Tie this in with a lesson on direct dialogue format by reviewing the rules for this type of writing beforehand, and then having each pair proofread, revise, and type a final draft before the presentations.*

PAIRING UP

Name:_____ Period:_____ Date:_____

Each of you has been assigned a character and a partner. Your pair will choose a situation from the literature we are studying. You and your partner will discuss the situation, the feelings, actions, and reactions of two characters involved in this situation, and then will write a dialogue that illustrates the characters' personalities, their involvement, and thoughts about the situation. You should write from the point of view of your assigned character. The views you present must show *your* analytical interpretations of this person and *not* those of the author. You will read these to the rest of the class when you are finished.

Character 1:_____ Character 2:_____

Situation: _____

_____

Dialogue: _____

_____

_____

_____

_____

_____

_____

_____

_____

_____

_____

_____

_____

_____

_____

_____

_____

_____

_____

_____

_____

_____

_____

TEACHER NOTES
Let's Tone Up

Bloom's Taxonomy

- Remember/Understand: name, explain, identify, describe
- Apply: draw, compose
- Analyze: infer, differentiate, distinguish, deduce
- Evaluate: conclude, decide, evaluate, give your opinion
- Create: hypothesize, imagine, suggest, suppose, compose

Common Core Standards

College and Career Readiness Anchor Standards, grades 6-9

Reading: RI, R2, R4, R6, RIO

Writing: WI, W2, W3, W4, W5, W9, WIO

Speaking & Listening: SLI, SL2, SL3, SL4

Language: LI, L2, L3, L5, L6

What: **Tone Analysis.**

When: Students will add to these sheets as they read. All five are due at the end of the reading.

Why: The tone of a story spawns visual, mental, and emotional reactions. Students need to understand that the characters' actions and reactions are a response to the tone of the situations. By doing so, they influence the character's choices as well as the situations the author included, thereby affecting the resolution.

How:

- Begin this lesson by writing the following topics on the board: *Movies*, *Books*, *TV Shows*, and *Lyrics*.

- Five students at a time should each write the title of an example under any of the headings along with one word to describe the overall tone/atmosphere. They should initial their responses.

- After all students have responded, lead a discussion by asking various students to explain their tone choices with supporting information; the more specific they are, the better it will be for the class to understand how writers create tone.

- Assign each student one of the tone adjectives. Ask them to think of a character from any novel who personifies this word and to explain how this attributed to the book's overall atmosphere/mood.

- Hand out five sheets to each student and explain that the students are to evaluate the tone that five characters exhibit in the story they are reading.

MORE ⟹

They are to complete all five sheets by the end of the reading—one each for the protagonist, the antagonist, and one for each of three other characters (students' choice).

- Explain that they will complete the Mile Run activity after they have finished reading the story.

LET'S TONE UP

All writers specifically choose words and sentence structures to convey their attitude or tone about the characters, their beliefs, as well as their actions and reactions. They make every word count to create a specific mood and atmosphere that changes with every scene. The way characters talk and act are meant to show their attitudes about themselves, about everyone they encounter, about their world, and about the lives that they lead. No matter how many moods mesh and collide, though, authors intend one tone to create an atmosphere for the whole piece.

Here are just a few words that may describe a character's attitude or tone:

Note: these words are all adjectives because they describe an aspect of the character's personality.

Indifferent	Bitter	Satirical	Happy	Insistent	Bold	Damning
Apprehensive	Incredulous	Silly	Terrified	Skeptical	Nostalgic	Interested
Disinterested	Sorrowful	Sneering	Serious	Joyful	Despairing	Joking
Disrespectful	Melodramatic	Subdued	Flirtatious	Arrogant	Objective	Demanding
Argumentative	Supportive	Upset	Apologetic	Furious	Cautious	Harsh

Now it's time to tone any brain flab with a few challenges.

Directions:

1. Warm-up:

Take five copies of this activity. Write the name of the protagonist, the antagonist, and three characters of your choice from this story, one character per copy.

2. Sit-up:

Write a paragraph explaining each person's role in the story and his/her general personality.

3. Sprint:

List three adjectives that describe the character's tone/mood from the beginning, middle, and end of the story that help create the overall atmosphere. Include a citation that shows this tone. Then, in a paragraph using supporting text, describe the overall tone/attitude that each character exhibits in the story.

4. Mile Run:

State the story's principal atmosphere and explain how the moods, the setting, and the characters' tones develop this quality. Include supporting text to develop your thesis statement.

LET'S TONE UP

Name:_____ Period:_____ Date:_____

Warm-up:
Character:_____

Sit-up:
Role in the story:_____

_____

_____

_____

Sprint:
Beginning adjective: _____

Citation:_____

_____

_____

_____

_____

Middle adjective:_____

Citation:_____

_____

_____

_____

_____

Ending adjective:_____

Citation:_____

_____

_____

_____

Character's Overall Tone:_____

_____

_____

_____

Name: _____

Mile Run:

State the story's principal atmosphere and explain how the moods, the setting, and the characters' tones develop this quality. Include supporting text.

_____

_____

_____

_____

_____

_____

_____

_____

_____

_____

_____

_____

_____

_____

_____

_____

_____

_____

_____

_____

_____

_____

_____

_____

_____

_____

_____

_____

_____

_____

_____

_____

CHAPTER 5

DECORATING

When the whole house is completed, what's left to do? Tie it all together. When a house is built, decorating brings each room together. When students have learned to analyze all the elements of literature, they need to know how to connect them all together.

Although an in-depth exploration of each of these elements will advance their comprehension levels, students must also understand how they intertwine with each other. This chapter's Story Review module provides opportunities for students to hear, read, think, write, speak, and do, which will help them maximize their learning.

The Story Review module includes activities that offer teachers substantial and comprehensive ways to assess their students' knowledge and understanding of how the elements of literature provide the structure for the textual material they study. There are activities for students to do individually, and ones that work well in a group or whole-class setting.

All the Story Review activities align to the same Common Core Standards and Bloom's Taxonomy terms. Teacher Notes for these activities are the same for all Story Review activities, except for the individual instructions for completing each activity.

STORY REVIEW MODULE

Individual Activities

- Character Collage
- Let the Music Live
- Analyze This!
- Comparing Books and Movies

Group or Whole-Class Activities

- Class Project: Newspaper
- SCORE with the Literature Super Bowl

TEACHER NOTES
Story Review Module

Bloom's Taxonomy

- **Remember/Understand:** name, explain, identify, describe
- **Apply:** illustrate, draw, compose
- **Analyze:** infer, examine, determine, deduce
- **Evaluate:** conclude, support, evaluate, select, give your opinion, justify
- **Create:** hypothesize, imagine, suggest, suppose, compose

Common Core Standards

College and Career Readiness Anchor Standards, grades 6-9

Reading: RI, R2, R3, R4, R5, R6, RIO

Writing: WI, W2, W3, W4, W5, W6, WIO

Speaking & Listening: SLI

What: Review of the elements of literature and their importance to story structure.

When: Present these activities after the reading is completed but before the final assessment on the literature.

Why: These activities offer a variety of projects that help students understand the importance of each element of literature to the whole piece.

How: See each activity for instructions. Grading rubrics follow on p. 146 for several activities.

For individual reinforcement and review:

- Character Collage

- Let the Music Live

- Analyze This!—*Although this activity was used as a pre-reading assessment, it is also beneficial as a post-reading assessment. By analyzing the results, you can see which elements of literature will need to be emphasized in future literature studies.*

- Comparing Books and Movies—*Make sure that students complete Part A **before** they view the movie. They complete Part B **after** they view the movie.*

For group reinforcement and review:

- Class Project: Newspaper

- SCORE with the Literature Super Bowl

Story Review Module Grading Rubrics

Character Collage:

Pictures..25%

Text...25%

Meeting Criteria...25%

Time and Effort...25%

Let the Music Live!:

Number of songs..50%

15 songs are required to receive the full point value for this segment. The teacher will determine the point value for any number less than 15.

Appropriateness of song choices......................25%

Why/How explanations for song choices............25%

Class Project: Newspaper:

Articles..50%

Layout...50%

(see detailed grading rubric for newspaper project)

CHARACTER COLLAGE

Directions:

Make a collage to show one character from the literature being studied.

Criteria:

- Cut out the first letter of the character's first name from a large (18" x 24") piece of poster board.

- Totally cover it with pictures (75%) and words (25%) that describe the character, setting, situations, conflicts, theme, and symbols, and any phrases that show these elements of literature.

- Text should be typed, carefully cut to fit, and glued on the poster board over the pictures.

- Make sure that your choices clearly represent and show the character.

- The poster board initial must be totally covered.

Example:

Character: Mollie (*Animal Farm* by George Orwell)

Types of items to glue on the collage:

ribbons, jewelry, horses, sugar lumps

Text to include (typed and sized to fit):

Vain, silly, materialistic, craved human attention,

"She took a place near the front and began flirting her mane,"

"Will there be sugar after the revolution?"

LET THE MUSIC LIVE!

Directions:

- Design, create, and burn a CD composed of music that shows the characters, setting, conflicts, theme, and tone of the book.
- Create a CD cover illustration. The lyrics for each piece chosen must be typed and sized to fit into a booklet that will fit behind the CD cover illustration.
- Burn the songs to a CD so segments can be played in class.
- On a separate sheet of paper, write a short explanation (one sentence for each title) relating:

  1. *Why* the song was chosen

  2. *How* it fits the scene/part of book that it accompanies

- Be sure to include the title and artist for each song.

ANALYZE THIS!
Novel/Short Story Review

Name:_____ Period:_____ Date:_____

Address each of the following points with specific facts, details, and examples from the story. Your answers will show how well you know and understand what you read. On the day of the review, be sure to bring up any areas where you need clarification.

1. Who is the protagonist? The antagonist? Name and identify other important characters.

Protagonist:_____

Antagonist:_____

Other characters:_____

2. Describe the setting/locale:

_____

_____

_____

3. What is the central conflict/problem that the protagonist is facing? Explain whether it is psychological, physical, emotional, spiritual, or a mixture of all of these issues.

_____

_____

_____

4. Describe three ways in which the protagonist's and antagonist's personalities are revealed (actions, reactions, words, other character's words, etc).

Protagonist:_____

_____

Antagonist:_____

_____

5. Reveal the five stages of the plot:

Exposition:_____

_____

_____

_____

Rising action (one complication per line): Give the complication, not the main character's responses.

_____

_____

_____

Climax:_____

_____

_____

_____

Name:_____

Falling action (one event per line):_____
_____
_____
_____

Resolution:_____
_____
_____
_____

6. Describe the tone/mood using a minimum of five specific adjectives or expressions:
_____
_____
_____
_____
_____

7. Give three symbols and explain what they represent.
    A._____
    B._____
    C._____

8. State the theme—the universal message that the author imparted. Explain how you derived this idea.
_____
_____
_____
_____
_____
_____
_____
_____
_____
_____
_____
_____
_____
_____
_____

COMPARING BOOKS AND MOVIES

Name:_____ Period:_____ Date:_____

Compare and contrast the book and the movie.

Part A:

Complete this part before viewing the movie.

1. What specific scenes do you look forward to seeing in the movie?

_____

_____

_____

_____

_____

_____

2. What specific places and sights do you expect to see in the movie?

_____

_____

_____

_____

_____

_____

3. Where would be a good setting to film this movie?

_____

_____

_____

_____

_____

_____

4. If you were making this movie, what would be your opening scene? What would be your closing scene?

_____

_____

_____

_____

_____

_____

Part B:

Complete this part after viewing the movie.

To answer #1 and #2, consider all of the elements of literature: characters, plot/conflict, setting, theme, symbols, tone, and point of view.

1. Similarities: _____
_____
_____
_____
_____
_____

2. Differences: _____
_____
_____
_____
_____
_____

3. Compare/contrast three of the characters in the book to their movie counterparts.
   A. _____
   B. _____
   C. _____

4. In what ways was the book better? _____
_____
_____
_____
_____

5. In what ways was the movie better? _____
_____
_____
_____
_____

CLASS PROJECT: NEWSPAPER
Teacher's Directions

Use this as a whole-class project or as a small-group project. For small groups, divide the students into groups of 5-7 students each. Your choice will depend on your goals for the class, as well as on the students' abilities and skill levels.

Students will create a newspaper with articles drawn from the events/characters in the book. They will include news stories, features, entertainment/style/review pieces, sports articles, obituaries, letters to the editor, and whatever else might be needed to complete the newspaper. Each student must include a visual with a caption to accompany his/her article as well as a printable headline.

1. On the first day of the unit, the teacher selects a student as editor-in-chief, as well as an editor for each section: news, features, sports, editorials, style/entertainment, etc. These students must be able to use a layout program such as InDesign, Publisher, or PageMaker, depending on what the school system has available.
   Note: consider extra credit for editors.

2. Students can either choose their own story idea or be assigned a topic by the teacher or editor as events occur or characters are developed.

3. All of the articles, visuals, and headlines must be turned in on the due date.

4. Headlines must be sentences, each with a specific subject and a strong active verb. Example: **Gangster Frequents East Egg Galas** (*The Great Gatsby*, F. Scott Fitzgerald)

5. Each writer lays out his/her own story, visual (picture, chart, or graphic to accompany each story), and headline. Section editors are responsible for the section's overall layout, completing or assigning for extra credit whatever might need to be done besides the assigned stories, (fillers, ads, cartoons, etc.) to utilize all of the space.

6. All editors must write an editorial or opinion piece. The editorial page must contain a masthead.

7. Every student in a section must peer critique all section pages.

8. Story requirements: See Student Directions

9. Teacher assigns number of pages, and number of major articles for each section depending on the number of students in the class. For a class of 25 students, articles could be assigned as follows: News (6), Features (4), Style/Entertainment (5), Sports (5), Editorials (5). The newspaper should be in multiples of four pages. A master chart is included on page **154**.

10. Grading: This project is worth 200 points. Articles are worth 100 points (50% of the project grade), and layout is worth 100 points (50% of the grade).

    Articles: Writers are responsible for writing five articles. Section editors and the editor-in-chief are responsible for writing one article each. The editor-in-chief must also write an editorial or opinion piece. These are all graded according to the Article Rubric on page **157**.

    Layout: Layout is graded according to the Layout Rubric on page **158**. There are separate layout rubrics for writers, section editors, and the editor-in-chief. Specific layout guidelines for grading are covered in the Student Directions on page **155**.

CLASS PROJECT NEWSPAPER MASTER CHART:

	Article/ Writer	Article/ Writer	Article/ Writer	Article/ Writer	Article/ Writer			
News Editor:								
Features Editor:								
Style/Entertainment Editor:								
Sports Editor:								
Editorials Editor:								

CLASS PROJECT: NEWSPAPER
Student Directions

The class will create a newspaper with articles drawn from the events/characters in the book. Include news stories, features, entertainment/style/review pieces, sports, obituaries, letters to the editor, and whatever else might be needed to complete the newspaper.

The teacher will choose a student as editor-in-chief, as well as an editor for each section. Editors must be able to use the chosen publishing program.

Section editors are responsible for their section's overall layout, completing or assigning for extra credit whatever might need to be done besides the assigned stories (fillers, ads, cartoons, etc). All editors must write an editorial or opinion piece. Section editors and the editor-in-chief must also write a story for the section of his/her choice.

1. Students choose their own story ideas or are assigned topics by the editor.
2. All of the articles, visuals, and headlines must be turned in on the due date.
3. Each writer will lay out his/her own story. Each story must include a visual (picture, chart, or graphic) with a caption to accompany the article, as well as a headline.
4. The teacher will assign the number of total pages and number of major articles for each section. See the master sheet to sign up when a topic inspires you as you read.
5. Every student in a section must peer critique all section pages.

Basic story requirements:

1. Lead paragraph: 30-35 words; body paragraphs: 35-45 words each.
2. Length: anywhere from 400-750 words, depending on the topic.
3. All articles are written in third person, except for the opinion/editorial pieces, which can be in first person. No second person may be used.
4. Each article should have a minimum of three quotes from "reliable" sources—i.e., other characters who would have "been there, seen that."
5. Each piece must reveal the time period in language, images, and societal attitudes, and must reflect the author's point of view.

Layout Guidelines:

- Point values for each requirement are shown below in parentheses.
- Photography: Photographer's/website's name under the graphic with the last letter of the last name even with the right-hand side of the picture. (Times New Roman, size 10, italicized). All photos in .tff format. All graphics/pictures should be proportional; do not stretch them. (20 points)
- Articles: Single-spaced, Times New Roman, size 10; byline italicized. Spacing 10. Justify all lines. Continued Format: "Continued on p. x" then "Continued from p. x," with an abbreviated headline. (30 points)
- Headlines: any font size; same font for all headlines on same page (although they can be

bold, italicized, or different size). Each headline must have a subject and a verb. Capitalize the first letter of each word. (10 points)

- Wrap text around pictures/graphics. (10 points)

- Center spread: must fill whole page. This must be in the exact middle so they appear side-by-side. Example: for a 20-page paper, the center should be pages 10 (left) and 11 (right). (10 points)

- Vary layouts: no two pages should be the same; there should not be any extra white space. (10 points)

- Bylines: name in bold and underlined; staff position italicized. (10 points)

CLASS NEWSPAPER PROJECT
Article Grading Rubric

Scoring
- 10 - Consistently meets/exceeds standards
- 9 - Mostly meets standards
- 8 - Vague research
- 7 - Frequent errors
- 6 - A multitude of errors

Article requirements	Score
Good research	
Meets editor-set word count	
Leads 30-35 words; paragraphs 30-35 words	
Proofread for spelling, punctuation, sentence structure, and taboo words and phrases	
Whole name used first time and then last name only	
Reads smoothly; facts, quotes, info are clearly presented	
Addresses the 5 Ws and H	
Meets all deadlines	
Dialogue explanatory remarks in past tense	
Visual w/caption and headline	
Total score for articles	

Maximum points for articles: 100
This project is worth 200 points. Articles comprise 50% of the grade and layout 50% of the grade.

CLASS NEWSPAPER PROJECT
Layout Grading Rubric - Writers

Writer's Name:_____

A. Article requirements:

5 articles = **100 points**

4 articles = **90 points**

3 articles = **80 points**

2 articles = **70 points**

1 article = **60 points**

Score:_____

B. Layout requirements (see Student Directions for specifics):

Photography _____

Articles _____

Headlines _____

Text wrap _____

Center spread _____

Variety of layouts _____

Bylines _____

Score:_____

C. Deadline requirements:

Deadline met = **100 points**

Late = **70 points**

Story or layout missing = **0**

Score:_____

Total Layout Score: (A + B + C) / 3 = _____

This project is worth 200 points.

Articles comprise 50% of the grade and layout 50% of the grade.

CLASS NEWSPAPER PROJECT
Layout Grading Rubric - Editors

Section Editor

Name:_____

A. Assigning extra articles = 20 points maximum

(Note: Make sure all white space is filled; assign extra pieces as needed.)

B. Overall layout = 40 points maximum

C. Deadline met = 40 points maximum

Score:_____

Total Layout Score: A + B + C = _____

Editor-in-Chief

Name:_____

A. Editorial (30 points) and Masthead (10 points) = 40 points maximum

B. Overall layout = 30 points maximum

C. Deadline = 30 points maximum

Score:_____

Total Layout Score: A + B + C = _____

This project is worth 200 points.

Articles comprise 50% of the grade and layout 50% of the grade.

SCORE WITH THE LITERATURE SUPER BOWL
Teacher's Directions

This game is a fun activity to motivate students during a review of a novel. The questions should test students' knowledge and understanding of the book as well as the literary elements discussed in class: Character, Plot, Conflict, Setting, Theme, Symbols, Point of View, and Tone/Mood.

Preparing the game:

1. Create questions about the novel. Gather the material that you want to review from study questions/guides, activities used during the study of the book, quizzes, and the final test. Make a numbered master list of your questions and a separate answer key, including each question's point value.

2. Each question's point value depends on the degree of difficulty. The harder the question, the higher the point value should be. Assign each question points following these guidelines:
   - 1 point (Extra Kick)
   - 2 points (Two-point Conversion)
   - 3 points (Field Goal)
   - 7 points (Touchdown)

3. Copy the sheet of football cards, creating as many football cards as you have questions on the material.

4. Cut out each question from the master list and glue it on the back of a football, along with the point value and its number on the answer key. When finished, copy this football sheet, double sided, as many times as needed. You will need as many sets of footballs as you have groups. Example: For a class of 25, divide the students into 5 groups of five students. Each group will then be divided into 2 teams of two players plus one referee (the person who reads the questions). With this configuration, you will need five sets of questions.

5. Laminate each sheet of football cards and cut them apart. Be sure to keep the sets separate.

6. Copy enough sets of answer keys to have one for each referee and one for you, and laminate them.

7. Label one each 3x5" index card: **Extra Kick, Two-Point Conversion, Field Goal,** and **Touchdown.** Make one set of index cards for every team.

8. Copy and laminate a spinner and arrow for each group.

9. Paste each spinner onto a piece of poster board cut to fit. Poke a hole in the rectangular end of each arrow and attach it to the center of a spinner, using a round-head fastener.

10. Divide the students into teams the day before the review so they can decide on a name and maybe choose to wear football jerseys to represent their teams. You could borrow referee jerseys from the athletic department for the referees to wear.

Playing the Game:

1. Divide students into groups with an equal number of students on each team within the group, and one student to act as the referee.

2. Give each referee a spinner and a score sheet.

3. Give each referee a set of football cards. Referee divides them into four piles on his/her desk: Extra Kick, Two-Point Conversion, Field Goal, and Touchdown, in front of each labeled index card (question-side down).

4. Have each referee read the directions (p. **165**).

5. Each referee will toss a coin to decide which team goes first.

6. Set a time limit, which will start when you blow the starting whistle.

7. The first team spins the arrow for the type of question.

8. The referee chooses a question from the stack of footballs with that point value and reads it.

9. Each team gets one minute to answer the question. When one minute has passed, the referee calls time and awards the team the number of points earned for the correct answer. Teams receive zero points for incorrect answers. (see attached score sheet)

10. The second team spins the arrow and the game continues as in steps 7, 8, and 9.

11. The game ends when the teacher calls time. The teams with the highest scores win.

TRY THIS

1. *Teachers can hold review sessions using this game throughout the unit, i.e., every X number of chapters. Playoffs can be held in 15-minute increments the day before the test, saving ten minutes for the Literature Super Bowl Championship. Students who have been knocked out of the game prior to this day may take turns as referees, and/or copy down the questions and answers for a study guide.*

2. *Football and referee jerseys, whistles, playing "We Are the Champions," and any other football-related accompaniments can be used for extra excitement!*

NOTE *This activity requires prep time, but it's worth doing. Approximate teacher time to create the game:*

- Type questions and answer key: 1 hour
- Glue one question on the back of each football with the point value: 30 minutes
- Copying and laminating the footballs, spinners/arrows, questions, and score sheets: 30 minutes
- Cut out the footballs and assemble the spinners: 15 minutes

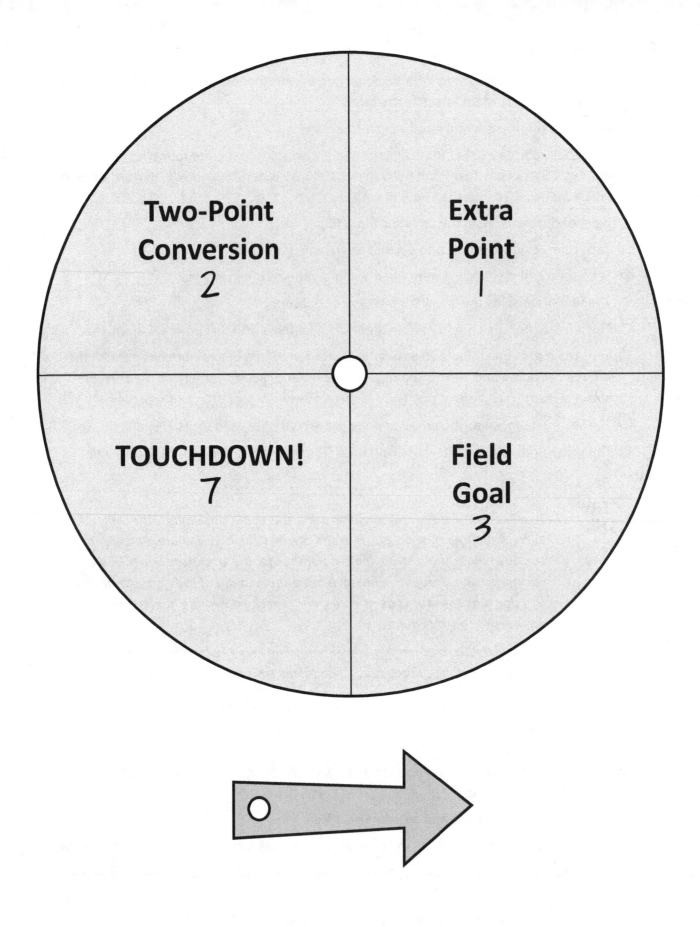

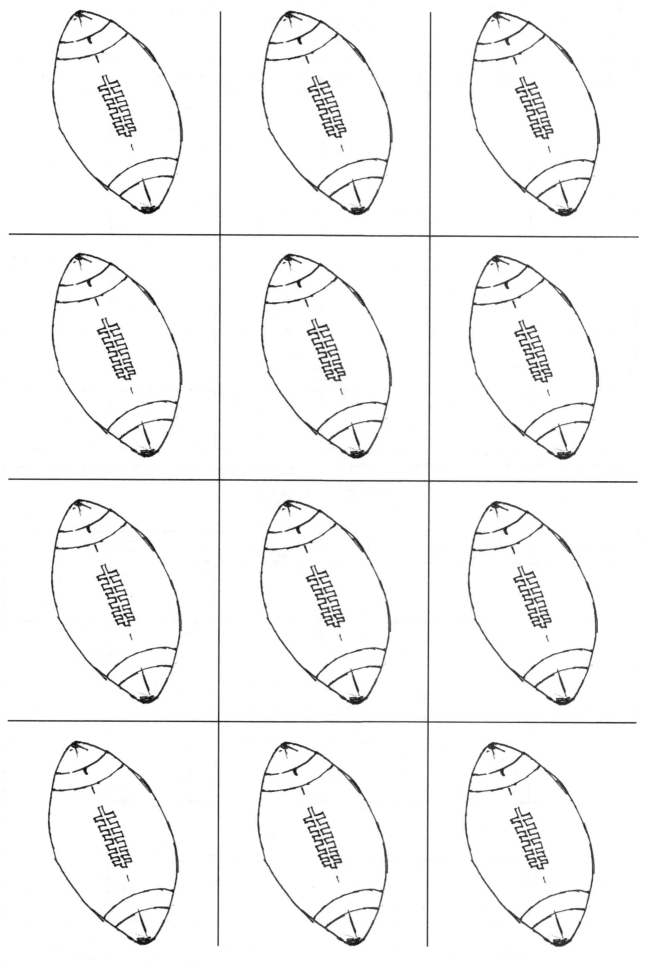

SCORE SHEET

Team Name	Extra Point (1)	Conversion (2)	Field Goal (3)	Touchdown (7)	Final Score

SCORE SHEET

Team Name	Extra Point (1)	Conversion (2)	Field Goal (3)	Touchdown (7)	Final Score

LITERATURE SUPER BOWL
HOW TO PLAY

1. The first team spins the arrow for the type of question.

2. The referee chooses a question from the stack of footballs with that point value and reads it.

3. Each team gets one minute to answer the question. When one minute has passed, the referee calls time and awards the team the number of points earned for the correct answer. Teams receive zero points for incorrect answers.

4. The second team spins the arrow and the game continues as in steps 1, 2, and 3.

5. The game ends when the teacher calls time. The team with the highest score wins.

CONCLUSION

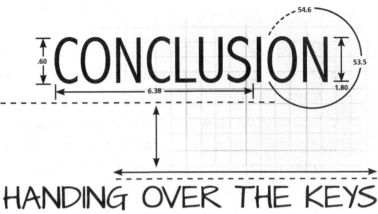

HANDING OVER THE KEYS

The *House of Comprehension* program provides teachers with a format that reveals the important partnership between the elements of literature and story structure. When English Language Arts teachers base every literature study on this concept, their students will successfully advance their comprehension levels, creating a firm academic foundation. More importantly, it equips learners with the skills, knowledge, and understanding that they need to be successful in the world outside of the classroom. If educators' overall objectives are to teach children to think, to teach children to express themselves orally and in writing, and to prepare them for the world outside of our schools, *The House of Comprehension* meets those goals.

Just decoding texts creates houses of straw and twigs—structures with no substance and durability. In order to erect a framework of knowledge and understanding that will withstand the huffing and puffing assaults of any literature study, students must arm themselves with tools and strategies.

The program in *The House of Comprehension* gives teachers a three-pronged approach:

Show Me:

The teacher presents lessons about the elements of literature and models how those elements create the story's structure.

Help Me:

The activities give students the chance to practice and exhibit what they are learning.

Let Me:

The discussions, projects, and assignments in the program allow students to synthesize their knowledge and understanding with their personal experiences and feelings.

With each piece of literature studied using these activities, teachers empower students to add depth and dimension to their comprehension of literature. At the end of the year, teachers can feel confident that their students, as active intellectual participants, have acquired the thinking, reasoning, and writing skills to take charge of their education. With the assurance that they have accomplished their academic goals, teachers can hand their students the keys to their own houses of comprehension.